Master Photo and Video Editing with Metal

A Practical Approach to Leveraging Metal Media Editing Software

Bogdan Redkin
Victor Yaskevich

Apress®

Master Photo and Video Editing with Metal: A Practical Approach to Leveraging Metal Media Editing Software

Bogdan Redkin
Buenos-Aires, Argentina

Victor Yaskevich
Warszawa, Poland

ISBN-13 (pbk): 979-8-8688-0831-9
https://doi.org/10.1007/979-8-8688-0832-6

ISBN-13 (electronic): 979-8-8688-0832-6

Managing Director, Apress Media LLC: Welmoed Spahr
Acquisitions Editor: Spandana Chatterjee
Desk Editor: James Markham
Editorial Project Manager: Kripa Joseph
Copyeditor: Kim Burton

Cover designed by eStudioCalamar

Cover image designed by Fancy Tech, LLC

Distributed to the book trade worldwide by Springer Science+Business Media New York, 1 New York Plaza, Suite 4600, New York, NY 10004-1562, USA. Phone 1-800-SPRINGER, fax (201) 348-4505, e-mail orders-ny@springer-sbm.com, or visit www.springeronline.com. Apress Media, LLC is a California LLC and the sole member (owner) is Springer Science + Business Media Finance Inc (SSBM Finance Inc). SSBM Finance Inc is a **Delaware** corporation.

For information on translations, please e-mail booktranslations@springernature.com; for reprint, paperback, or audio rights, please e-mail bookpermissions@springernature.com.

Apress titles may be purchased in bulk for academic, corporate, or promotional use. eBook versions and licenses are also available for most titles. For more information, reference our Print and eBook Bulk Sales web page at http://www.apress.com/bulk-sales.

Any source code or other supplementary material referenced by the author in this book is available to readers on GitHub. For more detailed information, please visit https://www.apress.com/gp/services/source-code.

If disposing of this product, please recycle the paper

Table of Contents

About the Authors

 **Bogdan Redkin** is an iOS developer with over ten years of experience creating top-notch iOS applications. As a founder of Fancy Tech, he launched multiple photo-editing solutions, achieving leading positions in the App Store. Having written many articles on *Medium* about drawing using Metal, he's decided to combine his passion for writing and GPU image processing by writing his first book.

 **Victor Yaskevich** is an experienced GPU programmer specializing in Vulkan, Metal, and shaders. With a strong focus on low-level graphics and system programming, he contributes his expertise to guide readers in mastering GPU programming and architecture patterns throughout this book.

Acknowledgments

Many thanks to those who supported me during my writing journey. I'm deeply indebted to my co-author, Victor, whose knowledge and expertise in GPU programming helped us create a book with more detail, depth, and value. Thanks goes to David, a wordsmith who shepherded me in the literary arts. Immense gratitude goes to my wife, Victoria, who always inspired and supported me throughout the entire process.

PART I

Rasterization

CHAPTER 1

Introduction

In a world increasingly driven by visual content, the ability to manipulate and enhance images and videos has become a must-have skill set for iOS engineers. More and more applications, including social networks, have built-in editing tools, with Apple consistently highlighting camera and photo app improvements at every event.

Achieving smooth image and video editing performance has never been so vital. Have you ever wondered how you could keep up with this or the capabilities of the Metal framework?

Welcome to *Mastering Photo and Video Editing with Metal*! This book teaches the art of image and video editing techniques, from simple color adjustment to complex filters and real-time video effects.

As you progress in your learning journey, each chapter provides a thorough theoretical explanation and real-world examples, with the final project containing essential instruments from modern photo editors (see Figure 1-1).

© Bogdan Redkin and Victor Yaskevich 2024
B. Redkin and V. Yaskevich, *Master Photo and Video Editing with Metal,*
https://doi.org/10.1007/979-8-8688-0832-6_1

Figure 1-1. *A screenshot of the final example project containing all the instruments explained in the book*

By the end of this book, you'll have an understanding of how to implement editing tools using Metal as well as being able to apply this knowledge to your own app by referencing to the final example project.

What Is Metal?

Metal is a low-level, unified, and low-overhead application programming interface (API) developed by Apple for utilizing the graphics processing unit (GPU). It provides near-direct access to the GPU, allowing for efficient rendering, parallel processing, and optimized use of the GPU's power. It is particularly suited for 3D graphics, data-parallel computation, gaming, video processing, machine learning, and image/video rendering applications.

In addition, it's also used in many of Apple's frameworks, including RealityKit, SceneKit, SpriteKit, and CoreImage.

History Overview

The story of GPU processing on Apple devices begins with the introduction of OpenGL for Macs in 1999, providing substantial graphics capability primarily for 3D gaming and professional applications. However, as the demand for more sophisticated graphics grew—especially with the advent of mobile computing—Apple recognized the need for a more optimized, low-overhead API that could maximize the performance of their hardware. This realization culminated in the launch of Metal in 2014 with iOS 8.

Unlike the previous solutions, Metal was designed specifically for Apple's Hardware with stunning results - up to 10x faster draw call rates! Furthermore, Metal offers developers revolutionary capabilities of computing GPU power and precompiled shaders.

Who Is This Book For?

You could be an intermediate Swift developer interested in photo and video editing or how GPU media processing works, for example.

You should have a basic knowledge of C++ or C, but it's not essential. However, you must use the Metal Shader Language in the GPU shader functions, which is based on C++.

How to Read This Book

Each chapter includes a starter project and explains one of the editing tools in detail. If you're already familiar with Metal on a basic level, you can jump to any tool, learn from a particular explanation of how the tool works, and compare your result with the final project.

However, beginners who haven't worked with the Metal framework should proceed from the start of the book.

Overview

- **Part I**: The book starts with the Metal fundamentals, understanding the rendering pipeline, core components, shader functions, and coordinate space. After that, you'll learn how to load custom images and convert them to metal textures. Then, you'll be introduced to transforming, rotating, and moving your textures.

- **Part II**: This part of the book explains how to apply such effects as color adjustments, including ones based on the lookup table, blur, and image distortion.

- **Part III**: Your journey accumulates all your learned knowledge and extends it to the possibility of applying image editing effects to layers and composing layers with different blend modes.

- **Part IV**: The final section builds on your knowledge of working with static images, introducing techniques of video editing with Metal by processing each frame with previously learned transformations and effects.

CHAPTER 2

Metal Fundamentals Overview: Rendering and Displaying Content

Your learning journey begins with the fundamentals of rendering with Metal.

This chapter begins with a theoretical introduction to components used for rendering content. You'll become familiar with the MetalKit framework, designed to simplify working with Metal by offering higher-level abstractions. After that, you get a quick introduction to concepts of the rendering pipeline and Metal's command submission model.

By the end of this chapter, you'll implement a rendering canvas with randomizing background color updates, as shown in Figure 2-1.

B. Redkin and V. Yaskevich, *Master Photo and Video Editing with Metal*,
https://doi.org/10.1007/979-8-8688-0832-6_2

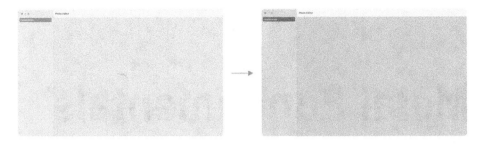

Figure 2-1. *The rendering canvas with randomizing background color updates*

Rendering

Rendering is the process of computing frame pixel colors through the GPU. The rendering result is the frame displayed on the screen.

The diagram shown in Figure 2-2 represents a sequence of events that leads to a rendered frame.

Figure 2-2. *The sequence of events that leads to a rendered frame*

1. **Initialize Metal**. Prepare MTKView or CAMetalLayer to display the result drawn with Metal on the screen. Set up the delegate for callbacks from MTKView.

2. **Prepare resources**. This chapter does not use external resources. However, later in this book, you will load textures, models, shader vertex, and fragment functions. This step is not part of a frame drawing loop and should be used only when the rendering pipeline state needs to be updated.

3. **Set up the pipeline.** Configure the rendering pipeline state with prepared resources.

4. **Render.** Set the configured rendering pipeline stat for the render command encoder. Then, if any of the shader functions can receive arguments, the encoder is updated with new data from the buffer or a texture.

This is a highly generalized description of the rendering in metal to make the first acquaintance smoother. In more complex applications, each of these events has more stages and operations underneath, and later in this book, you'll decompose and explore them in more detail.

GPU Devices

MTLDevice represents an abstraction of the GPU and serves as the primary entry point for your app's interaction.

An MTLDevice instance is required to access anything from the GPU. Therefore, essential classes such as MTLRenderPipelineState, MTKView, and MTLCommandQueue require either a metal device instance or a different class that contains it.

Getting a GPU Device

To get a default Metal device, call the MTLCreateSystemDefaultDevice() function. If there is only one GPU, such as those in iOS devices, you can always use the default device.

```
let device = MTLCreateSystemDefaultDevice()!
```

The system default is the discrete GPU on macOS devices with multiple GPUs.

Buffers

MTLBuffer represents a typeless, general-purpose memory allocation that sends and retrieves data from a shader function. Buffers are universal, capable of holding anything from vertex data to texture information, which the GPU then uses to perform rendering tasks.

Buffer Creation

To create a buffer, you need to call a makeBuffer(length:options:) function from the current instance of the Metal device.

```
let buffer = device.makeBuffer(length: 16, options: [])
```

In this example, you specified a 16-byte memory allocation.

If you need to create the buffer from existing data and calculate the allocation size, use the makeBuffer(bytes:length:options:) method.

```
var matrix: matrix_float4x4 = matrix_float4x4([1, 0, 0, 0],
                                              [0, 1, 0, 0],
                                              [0, 0, 1, 0],
                                              [0, 0, 0, 1])
let buffer = device.makeBuffer(
                bytes: &matrix,
                length: MemoryLayout<matrix_float4x4>.stride,
                options: [])
```

With MemoryLayout, you can get the allocation size from any variable.

Commands to the GPU

A Metal device instance provides GPU access, but how do you process something on the GPU?

To process something on GPU, you need to find a way to communicate with it, and communication between Metal apps and the GPU on a device works through commands that instruct the GPU to perform drawing, computation, or resource management operations.

You wrap these commands in a command encoder and encapsulate them in a command buffer. Then, a command queue submits a batch of command buffers to the GPU.

Figure 2-3 illustrates two command encoders; the second is an example of a render command encoder with a couple of render-specific commands.

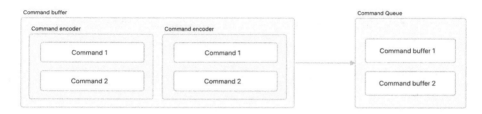

Figure 2-3. *Two command encoders*

Command Queue

A **command queue** is an object that conforms to the MTLCommandQueue protocol. This object manages a queue of command buffers. An app creates command buffers from this queue and submits them to the GPU for execution. The command queue ensures that submitted command buffers are executed in a FIFO (First In, First Out) order.

To create a command queue, use the following code.

```
guard
    let commandQueue = device.makeCommandQueue()
else { return }
```

The device and the command queue are instances that stay alive for the duration of the app's session, so you must use the same command queue as the device it was created.

Create a Command Buffer

When the queue is just created, it's empty. To submit commands to the GPU, you must commit a new command buffer to the command queue on each frame.

The following code creates a command buffer.

```
guard
    let commandBuffer = commandQueue.makeCommandBuffer()
else { return }
```

At this point, you have a command buffer ready to write commands into.

Encode Commands

The process of writing commands into a command buffer is called **encoding**. Commands are encoded into command buffers using either MTLRenderCommandEncoder for rendering tasks or MTLComputeCommandEncoder for computing tasks.

When you call a function provided by the command encoder—like draw or compute operations—the encoder inserts commands corresponding to those calls into the command buffer, including everything the GPU needs to process the task at runtime.

Figure 2-4 illustrates the two command encoders that insert commands into a command buffer.

- **Render command encoders** for draw commands: You will use render passes in the next chapter.

- **Compute command encoders** for compute functions: The compute function is one of the key components in photo and video editing applications.

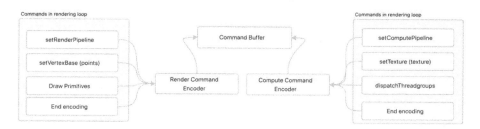

Figure 2-4. *Two command encoders inserting commands into a command buffer*

When you're finished writing commands with a command encoder, you need to finalize the result by calling the endEncoding() method of the command encoder.

Submit Commands

To submit your commands to run on the GPU, you must commit a command buffer, which lets its associated command queue know it's ready for execution.

```
commandBuffer.commit()
```

You now know how to encode and submit commands for the GPU. Let's get acquainted with the MTKView class, which allows you to display the rendering result.

MTKView

The MTKView class inherits from the base view classes on both platforms—from NSView on macOS and UIView on iOS. You can manage the layout of this view similar to a regular UIView. Under the hood, MTKView uses a CAMetalLayer to display the rendered results.

MTKView renders a texture for every frame, so it requires an instance of MTLDevice to access a GPU.

```
var metalView = MTKView()
metalView.device = device
```

Another MTKView property is used in this chapter: clearColor.

```
metalKitView.clearColor = Color.random.mtlColor
```

The MTKViewDelegate

MTKView has an MTKViewDelegate, offering a convenient way to respond to draw requests and render new textures.

The delegate is required to implement two methods.

- mtkView(_:drawableSizeWillChange:) is called by the view when the size changes.

- draw(in:) is called by the view whenever a new frame needs to be drawn. It is where you submit commands to GPU.

That's it. You've been introduced to all fundamental Metal components, so let's practice your new knowledge.

Starter Project

Let's begin!

1. Clone the resources repository if you haven't cloned it yet.

2. Open a starter project from the folder named 02_fundamentals and jump into a class named MetalView.

As you can see, MTKView doesn't have a native implementation in SwiftUI yet, so you need to implement it yourself.

```
import SwiftUI
import MetalKit

struct MetalView: View {
  @State private var metalView = MTKView()
  @State private var renderer: Renderer?

  var body: some View {
    MetalViewRepresentable(metalView: $metalView)
      .onAppear {
        renderer = Renderer(metalView: metalView)
      }
  }
}

#if os(macOS)
typealias ViewRepresentable = NSViewRepresentable
#elseif os(iOS)
typealias ViewRepresentable = UIViewRepresentable
#endif

struct MetalViewRepresentable: ViewRepresentable {
```

```
  @Binding var metalView: MTKView

  #if os(macOS)
  func makeNSView(context: Context) -> some NSView {
    metalView
  }
  func updateNSView(_ uiView: NSViewType, context: Context) {
    updateMetalView()
  }
  #elseif os(iOS)
  func makeUIView(context: Context) -> MTKView {
    metalView
  }

  func updateUIView(_ uiView: MTKView, context: Context) {
    updateMetalView()
  }
  #endif

  func updateMetalView() { }
}

struct MetalView_Previews: PreviewProvider {
  static var previews: some View {
    VStack {
      MetalView()
    }
  }
}
```

The MTKViewDelegate class is implemented in the Renderer class.

The Renderer class is a custom class responsible for handling rendering requests from the MTKView class. In this chapter, you set up the foundation of this class by basic configuration of the command encoder and the command buffer. Later, you use the Renderer class as a starting point for the modifications described in the rendering pipeline.

Let's implement the Renderer class.

1. Open a file named Renderer and add an update it with a few class variables and updated init method from the following code.

```
private var device: MTLDevice
private var metalKitView: MTKView

// The current size of the view used as an input to the
vertex shader.
private var viewportSize: CGSize

// The command queue is used to pass commands to
the device.
private var commandQueue: MTLCommandQueue?

init(metalView mtkView: MTKView) {
    self.device = MTLCreateSystemDefaultDevice()!
    mtkView.device = self.device
    mtkView.preferredFramesPerSecond = 120
    self.metalKitView = mtkView
    self.viewportSize = mtkView.drawableSize
    super.init()

    // Each frame when we get a texture to render to,
    // it will have that color.
```

```
        metalKitView.clearColor = Color.white.mtlColor

        // Create the command queue
        commandQueue = device.makeCommandQueue()
    }
```

This code configures the Renderer class with a provided instance of MTKView. The initialized device variable is a single created instance of the MTLDevice class during all rendering iterations. The viewportSize variable sets a viewport area of the render encoder. commandQueue needs to store a command buffer for the next rendering pass.

2. Set the Renderer class as an implementation of MTKViewDelegate and update init by providing the Renderer instance as a delegate to mtkView.

```
    class Renderer: NSObject, MTKViewDelegate {

        init(metalView mtkView: MTKView) {
            ...
            // Set MTKViewDelegate
            metalKitView.delegate = self
        }
    }
```

3. Implement the required MTIViewDelegate methods: draw(in:) and mtkView(:drawableSizeWill Change:).

```
    /// Called whenever view changes orientation or
    is resized
        func mtkView(_ view: MTKView, drawableSizeWill
        Change size: CGSize) {
```

```
    // Save the size of the drawable to pass to the
    vertex shader.
    viewportSize = size
}

/// Called whenever the view needs to render
a frame.
func draw(in view: MTKView) {
    guard
        // Create a new command buffer for each
        render pass to the current drawable.
        let commandBuffer = commandQueue?.
        makeCommandBuffer(),
        // Obtain a renderPassDescriptor generated
        from the view's drawable textures
        let renderPassDescriptor = view.current
        RenderPassDescriptor,
        // Create a render command encoder.
        let renderEncoder = commandBuffer.make
        RenderCommandEncoder(descriptor:
        renderPassDescriptor)
    else { return }

    // Set the region of the drawable to draw into.
    renderEncoder.setViewport(MTLViewport(
        originX: .zero,
        originY: .zero,
        width: Double(viewportSize.width),
        height: Double(viewportSize.height),
        znear: .zero,
        zfar: 1.0
    ))
```

```
if ((Date().timeIntervalSince1970 * 1000)
.int % 95 == .zero) {
    // Generate random background color.
    metalKitView.clearColor = Color.random.
    mtlColor
}

renderEncoder.endEncoding()

// Schedule a present once the framebuffer is
complete using the current drawable.
commandBuffer.present(view.currentDrawable!)

// Finalize rendering here & push the command
buffer to the GPU.
commandBuffer.commit()
}
```

Let's discuss what's happening.

- MTKViewDelegate was implemented for metalKitView, and since then metalKitview has started to call draw(in:) every time a new frame needs to be drawn as well as mtkView(:drawableSizeWillChange:) every time the drawable size of metalKitView changes.

- According to your implementation of mtkView(:drawableSizeWillChange:), it updates the viewportSize, which is used for updating the drawable region size.

- In draw(in:), you obtain a reference to the view's render pass descriptor, which describes how the rendering should be carried out based on the current drawable textures. The renderPassDescriptor creates a render command encoder, which encodes rendering commands into the command buffer.

- Then, based on the current time, every 95 milliseconds, a random background color is generated for `metalKitView`.

- When you're done with `renderEncoder`, `renderEncoder.endEncoding()` finalizes all updates.

- When all the `renderEncoder` updates are finished, `commandBuffer` schedules a present operation to display the rendered frame using the current drawable texture and commit all the changes.

Build and run the example project. Select the Fundamentals lesson in the navigation list. You should see the updates of the background color, as shown in Figure 2-5.

Figure 2-5. *The final version of the example project*

Conclusion

In this chapter, you learned the basic components provided by the Metal framework to simplify the rendering process. In the next chapter, you learn about the rendering pipeline.

CHAPTER 3

The Rendering Pipeline

The previous chapter introduced you to the basics of rendering. This chapter provides a more detailed explanation of how graphics are processed and rendered. Specifically, you explore the intermediate stages in the rendering process.

- The rendering pipeline

- Coordinate spaces

- Vertex and fragment shader functions

What happens after the command buffer is committed? How do submitted commands transform into rendered pixels? Let's figure it out.

The Rendering Pipeline

The graphics rendering pipeline is a structured sequence of operations during which vertices data is drawn in the output texture.

This process is similar to an assembly line in a factory, where different stages contribute sequentially to the final product. In this case, the pipeline receives a set of GPU commands that detail the rendering process. The result is rendered pixels composed onto the output texture.

© Bogdan Redkin and Victor Yaskevich 2024
B. Redkin and V. Yaskevich, *Master Photo and Video Editing with Metal*,
https://doi.org/10.1007/979-8-8688-0832-6_3

So, to customize the final rendered result, you must customize one of these intermediate rendering steps.

The diagram shown in Figure 3-1 represents this "assembly line."

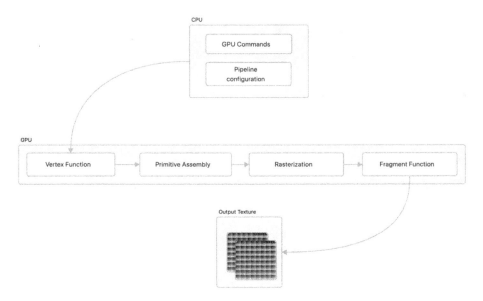

Figure 3-1. *The rendering pipeline*

Chapter 2 introduced the foundational components involved in command creation and submission. However, that chapter didn't cover GPU commands' customizing possibilities. So, before exploring the pipeline itself, let's have a quick overview of what kind of data it could receive and how this data affects the rendering pipeline.

Pipeline State

MTLRenderingPiplineState is an interface that controls how the graphics are processed and rendered. Specifically, the pipeline state controls which shader functions and what rasterization and tessellation is used during a render pass.

To make an instance of the `MTLRenderingPiplineState` protocol, you need another class, `MTLRenderPipelineDescriptor`, which is a container for all the configuration options of the pipeline state.

The following is sample code for pipeline state creation.

```
let pipelineDescriptor = MTLRenderPipelineDescriptor()
pipelineDescriptor.vertexFunction = vertexFunction
pipelineDescriptor.fragmentFunction = fragmentFunction
//..
let pipelineState = try? device.makeRenderPipelineState
(descriptor: pipelineDescriptor)
```

In the code, the vertex and fragment shader functions are specified. During the next render pass, these **shader functions** determine the position and color of each vertex.

What Are Shader Functions?

Shader functions, often called **shaders**, are specialized programs designed to run on a GPU. Shaders are a restricted programming model with their own language and functionality, that's to say, designed for the parallelism of GPUs and to mesh with the graphics pipeline well.

Metal Shading Language

Shaders for Metal are written in Metal Shading Language (MSL). This is a derivative of C++ designed specifically for GPU tasks, enabling precise control over graphics processing and computation.

There are several types of shader functions in Metal. This chapter covers two parts of the rendering pipeline: vertex shader function and fragment shader function.

The **vertex shader function** is a function that runs once for every vertex drawn. It's responsible for calculating the position of each vertex in a coordinate space.

```
vertex float4 shaderVertex(
        device float2 const* positions [[buffer(0)]],
                        uint vertexID [[vertex_id]]) {
    float2 position = positions[vertexID]; return float4
    (position, 0.0, 1.0);
}
```

Example of a basic vertex shader. It returns the same 2D position as it received.

The **fragment shader function** uses the variables that come from the vertex shader. It is executed once per pixel, which each drawn primitive type covers. Its responsibility is to output the final color.

```
fragment float4 shaderFragment(float4 position [[stage_in]]) {
        return float4(1.0, 0.0, 0.0, 1.0);
}
```

Example of a basic fragment shader function. It returns a solid red color.

GPU Commands

If the pipeline state is focused on the rendering pipeline configuration, GPU commands are otherwise responsible for the actions during a frame rendering loop. There are two types of commands in the rendering pipeline.

- **Resource preparation commands** assign resource data to one of the shader functions.

    ```
    encoder.setVertexBuffer(buffer, offset: 0, index: 0)
    ```

- **Drawing commands** send requests to draw something from the vertices that passed earlier.

```
encoder.drawPrimitives(type: .triangle, vertexStart:
.zero, vertexCount: vertices.count)
```

Now that you've had an overview of all the components in the configuration of the rendering pipeline, let's practice this knowledge and render a triangle.

Render a Triangle

First, let's overview the starter project. The primary update is a new RenderingTool protocol.

```
protocol RenderingTool {
    var device: MTLDevice { get }

    func handleRenderEncoder(encoder: MTLRenderCommandEncoder,
    metalView mtkView: MTKView, viewportSize: CGSize)

}
```

The RenderingTool protocol describes the generic MTLRenderCommandEncoder. Each new tool in the example app implements this method with custom handling depending on the needs of a particular tool.

With this update, you only need to implement this protocol and link it in a related view class to create a new tool. Take a look at this code from the previous lesson updated as an implementation of the RenderingTool protocol.

```
class FundamentalsRenderingTool: RenderingTool {
    private(set) var device: MTLDevice

    init() {
```

27

```
        self.device = MTLCreateSystemDefaultDevice()!
    }

    func handleRenderEncoder(encoder: MTLRenderCommandEncoder,
    metalView mtkView: MTKView, viewportSize: CGSize) {
        // Set the region of the drawable to draw into.
        encoder.setViewport(MTLViewport(
            originX: .zero,
            originY: .zero,
            width: Double(viewportSize.width),
            height: Double(viewportSize.height),
            znear: .zero,
            zfar: 1.0
        ))

        if ((Date().timeIntervalSince1970 * 1000).int
        % 95 == .zero) {
            // Generate a random background color.
            mtkView.clearColor = Color.random.mtlColor
        }
    }
}
```

Build and run a starter project. You should have the same results as the previous project (see Figure 3-2).

Figure 3-2. *The result of compiling the starter project*

Create a Render Pipeline State

The pipeline state configures the rendering pipeline. Let's create it.

1. Open the RenderingPipelineRenderingTool.
    swift file. Update it with a new function,
    createPipelineStateIfNeeded, and a
    corresponding class variable to store the configured
    pipeline state.

    ```
    class RenderingPipelineRenderingTool: RenderingTool {
        private(set) var device: MTLDevice
        private var pipelineState: MTLRenderPipelineState?

        init() {
            self.device = MTLCreateSystemDefaultDevice()!
        }
    ```

29

```
func handleRenderEncoder(encoder:
MTLRenderCommandEncoder, metalView mtkView:
MTKView, viewportSize: CGSize) {
    createPipelineStateIfNeeded(metalView: mtkView)
}

private func createPipelineStateIfNeeded(metalView
mtkView: MTKView) {
    guard self.pipelineState == nil else { return }
    // Load all the shader files with a .metal file
    extension in the project.
    let defaultLibrary = device.makeDefault
    Library()

    // Load functions from the library.
    let vertexFunction = defaultLibrary?.
    makeFunction(name: "shaderVertex")
    let fragmentFunction = defaultLibrary?.
    makeFunction
    (name: "shaderFragment")

    // Configure a pipeline descriptor that is used
    to create a pipeline state.
    let pipelineDescriptor = MTLRenderPipeline
    Descriptor()
    pipelineDescriptor.rasterSampleCount = mtkView.
    sampleCount
    pipelineDescriptor.vertexFunction = vertexFunction
    pipelineDescriptor.fragmentFunction =
    fragmentFunction
    pipelineDescriptor.colorAttachments[0].
    pixelFormat = mtkView.colorPixelFormat
```

```
do {
    self.pipelineState = try device.
    makeRenderPipeline
    State(descriptor: pipelineDescriptor)
} catch {
    // Pipeline State creation could fail
    if the pipeline descriptor isn't set up
    properly.
    //  If the Metal API validation is enabled,
        you can find out more information
        about what
    //  went wrong. (Metal API validation
        is enabled by default when a debug
        build is run
    //  from Xcode.)
    assertionFailure("Failed to create pipeline
    state: \(error)")
    }
  }
}
```

The createPipelineStateIfNeeded function in the
RenderingPipelineRenderingTool class sets up the rendering pipeline
state, which controls how the graphics are processed and rendered. Here's
how it works.

1. Load the shader functions. First, the function loads
   shader functions from the default library.

2. Configure the pipeline descriptor. It creates an
   MTLRenderPipelineDescriptor object, which has
   properties that describe the graphic rendering
   pipeline state you want to use during the
   rendering pass.

3. Create a pipeline state. Using the configured descriptor, it creates the pipeline state. This step might fail if the descriptor isn't set up correctly.

Create Shader Functions

By successfully creating the pipeline state, you defined what shader functions are and how they are used in the rendering process. However, shader functions are not yet implemented. Put the following code in the Shader.metal file to create the vertex and fragment functions.

```
struct Vertex {
    float4 position [[position]];
    float4 color;
};

vertex Vertex shaderVertex(constant Vertex *vertices [[
buffer(0) ]], uint vid [[ vertex_id ]]) {
    Vertex out = vertices[vid];

    float2 pos = float2(out.position.x, out.position.y);
    out.position = float4(pos, 0, 1);
    return out;
};

fragment half4 shaderFragment(Vertex input [[ stage_in ]]) {
    return half4(input.color);
};
```

Now that the rendering pipeline is configured, you need to declare the data to render. Let's create an equivalent structured model in Swift. To do so, create a new Vertex.swift file in the Models folder with the following code.

```
import Foundation
import simd
import SwiftUI

struct Vertex {
    var position: vector_float4
    var color: vector_float4

    init(position: vector_float4, color: vector_float4) {
        self.position = position
        self.color = color
    }

    init(x: CGFloat, y: CGFloat, color: Color) {
        self.init(position: vector_float4(Float(x), Float(y),
        0, 1), color: color.vectorFloat4)
    }
}
```

This structure works like a bridge between Swift data types from the CoreGraphics and MSL vectors, making it easier to initialize a vertex structure.

Set the Render Pipeline Resources, and Drawing Command

Let's continue the implementation of the RenderingPipelineRenderingTool class by updating the handleRenderEncoder method.

```
guard let pipelineState else { return }
encoder.setRenderPipelineState(pipelineState)
```

```
// Set the region of the drawable to draw into.
encoder.setViewport(MTLViewport(
    originX: .zero,
    originY: .zero,
    width: Double(viewportSize.width),
    height: Double(viewportSize.height),
    znear: .zero,
    zfar: 1.0
))

let vertices = [
    Vertex(x: 0.25, y: -0.25, color: .green),
    Vertex(x: -0.25, y: -0.25, color: .red),
    Vertex(x: 0.0, y: 0.25, color: .blue)
]

let buffer = device.makeBuffer(
    bytes: vertices,
    length: (MemoryLayout<Vertex>.stride * vertices.count) * 2,
    options: .storageModeShared
)
// Pass in the parameter data.
encoder.setVertexBuffer(buffer, offset: 0, index: 0)

// Draw the points primitives
encoder.drawPrimitives(type: .triangle, vertexStart: .zero,
vertexCount: vertices.count)
```

The handleRenderEncoder function is responsible for encoding rendering instructions for Metal to execute. This function is called when you're ready to render frames.

The following describes how to render frames.

1. Ensure that you have a valid pipeline state (guard let pipelineState = pipelineState else { return }) because you can't render without it.

2. Set the current pipeline state using encoder.setRe nderPipelineState(pipelineState), telling Metal which rendering pipeline to use.

3. Define the data, such as vertex positions and colors. In this case, there are three points for the vertices of the triangle.

4. Create a buffer to pass this data to the vertex function.

5. Pass the data to the vertex function using encoder.setVertexBuffer(...), making it available for the shader to use.

6. Draw the point primitives using encoder.drawPrimitives(...), specifying the type of primitive, the starting vertex, and the number of vertices to draw.

7. Build and run the project. The result is shown in Figure 3-3.

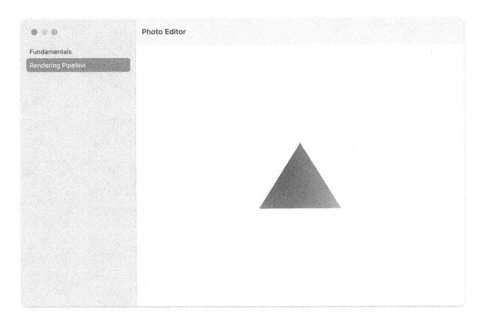

Figure 3-3. *A rendered a triangle at the center of the screen*

As you can see, we have successfully rendered a triangle at the center of the screen. Now, let's take a closer look at the stages of the rendering pipeline.

Rendering Pipeline Stages Overview

The source code from the previous example described only the configuration part, but what happened after the `drawPrimitives` command was executed? According to the rendering pipeline diagram shown in Figure 3-4, none of these stages are responsible for rendering the final result.

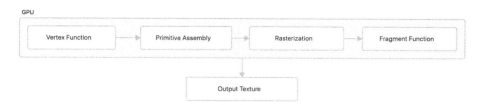

Figure 3-4. *Stages of the rendering pipeline responsible for rendering the final result*

Vertex Function

Let's discuss the first stage where the vertex shader function is executed. In your example, the shaderVertex function in Metal takes vertex data (positions and colors) and returns the exact position of each vertex, but now it's converted to clip-space coordinates. Figure 3-5 represents this stage.

However, the vertex function is capable of computing more complex position transformations. These capabilities are further explored later in the book.

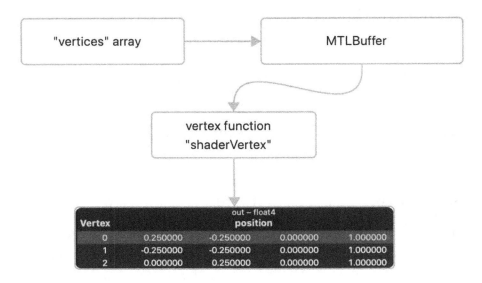

Figure 3-5. *Calculation of the vertices' position during the first stage of the rendering pipeline*

Primitive Assembly

After vertices are processed, the primitive assembly stage collects and assembles them into a geometric primitive—in this case, a triangle (see Figure 3-6).

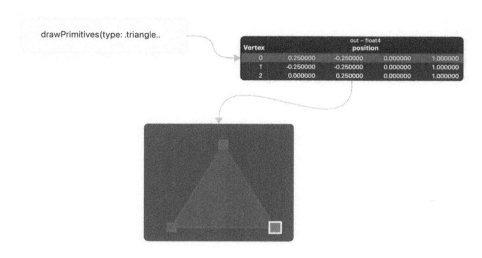

Figure 3-6. *Mapping vertices into primitive*

Rasterization

This stage includes converting the triangle from vector graphics (shapes defined by vertices and lines) into raster graphics (a set of pixels). Here, the GPU determines which pixels inside the triangle's boundaries are affected by the drawing command. This involves interpolating vertex attributes (like color) across the triangle to be used in the next stage (see Figure 3-7).

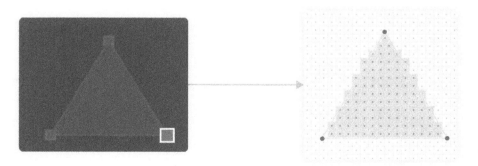

Figure 3-7. *How to convert a primitive from a vector into raster graphics by filling pixels inside its boundaries*

39

Fragment Function

This function runs for every pixel that needs to be drawn (as determined by the rasterization stage). It takes the interpolated vertex colors and outputs the final color for each pixel within the triangle (see Figure 3-8).

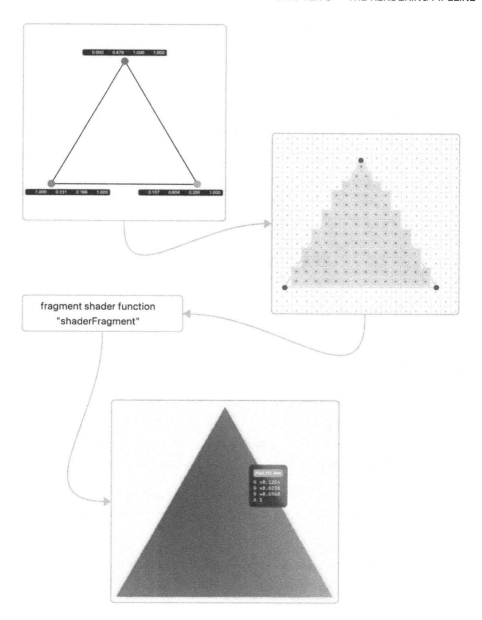

Figure 3-8. *Calculation of the final color of each pixel*

The Output Texture

The result of these steps is shown in Figure 3-9, a rendered triangle filled with a gradient containing interpolated colors between vertices.

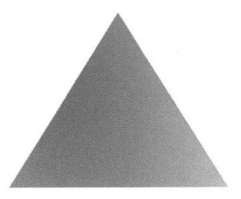

Figure 3-9.   *The rendering result*

Conclusion

In this chapter, you became familiar with how graphics are processed and rendered. You gathered a basic understanding of the intermediate stages in the rendering process: rendering pipeline, coordinate space, and vertex and fragment shader functions. The following are some other key points.

- The graphics rendering pipeline is a series of operations that transform vertex data into pixels in the output texture.

- The pipeline state controls the shader functions and the type of rasterization and tessellation used during a render pass.

- Shader functions are written in MSL and run on the GPU.

- Vertex and fragment shaders are part of the rendering pipeline. The vertex shader calculates the position of each vertex in the clip coordinate space, and the fragment shader outputs the final color.

- GPU commands are responsible for actions during a frame rendering loop, including resource preparation and drawing commands.

- The rendering pipeline stages include the vertex function, primitive assembly, rasterization, and fragment function.

CHAPTER 4

The Vertex Shader Function and Primitive Assembly

Chapter 3 explored the rendering pipeline, the roles of its stages, and how to render a triangle. This chapter discusses the vertex function topics, including supported attributes, coordinate spaces and transformations, coordinate spaces, and primitive types.

Vertex Function Attributes

During your practice with the rendering pipeline, you created your first vertex function, which received two parameters: a pointer to a buffer containing the Vertex structure and a vertex_id. The return type of the vertex function is the same Vertex structure as received in the input.

```
struct Vertex {
    float4 position [[position]];
    float4 color;
};
```

© Bogdan Redkin and Victor Yaskevich 2024
B. Redkin and V. Yaskevich, *Master Photo and Video Editing with Metal*,
https://doi.org/10.1007/979-8-8688-0832-6_4

```
vertex Vertex shaderVertex(constant Vertex *vertices [[
buffer(0) ]], uint vid [[ vertex_id ]]) {
....
```

Next, let's look at the attributes available for vertex function inputs and outputs, examining how each affects the rendering process.

Input Attributes

Each input argument of the vertex function can be specified with an attribute qualifier. These qualifiers are required to identify the source of the argument data.

For example, the attribute [[vertex_id]] indicates that the corresponding argument is the per-vertex identifier, which you can use to access specific vertex attributes from an array of vertex data. The following line shows that this identifier can address the current buffer data.

```
Vertex out = vertices[vid];
```

The [[vertex_id]] attribute is one of the built-in attributes, meaning it is automatically generated and assigned by the Metal API. You can find the complete list of built-in attributes in Table 5.2 of the MSL Specification (see https://developer.apple.com/metal/Metal-Shading-Language-Specification.pdf#page=99).

Another type of input argument attribute is specified to identify the location for these argument types.

- Buffers: [[buffer(index)]]

- Textures: [[texture(index)]]

- Samplers: [[sampler(index)]]

- Threadgroup buffers: [[threadgroup(index)]]

For example, during your practice with the rendering pipeline, you submitted the rendering data by using encoder. setVertexBuffer(buffer, offset: 0, index: 0), then you declare it as an argument in the vertex function with this code *vertices [[buffer(0)]].

Output Attributes

In the return type, there is only one attribute you should be aware of: [[position]].

The [[position]] attribute is required if the vertex function return type is a structure. Otherwise, the vertex function's return type must be float4.

The [[position]] attribute is required if the vertex function's return type is a structure that includes a position. Otherwise, the return type could also be a different structure or float4, depending on what is being output.

For example, let's look at the Vertex structure, which is declared a vertex function result type.

```
struct Vertex {
    float4 position [[position]];
    float4 color;
};
```

47

The Vertex structure includes two variables.

- **color** is a float4 data type, a simple type with four float numbers (RGBA) representing color.

- **position** is another float4 variable, but it contains coordinates in a 4D homogeneous vector format (x, y, z, w). (Metal coordinate spaces are discussed later.) The position variable is labeled with an attribute qualifier [[position]] to indicate that it represents the vertex position and should be written to the output buffer.

More information about these attribute qualifiers is in Table 5.3 of the MSL Specification (see https://developer.apple.com/metal/Metal-Shading-Language-Specification.pdf#page=97).

Coordinate Space and Transformations in Vertex Functions

The main purpose of a vertex function is to determine the position of each vertex. However, during your practice with the rendering pipeline, the vertex's input position was defined in clip space coordinates, so they don't require additional transformations.

```
let vertices = [
    Vertex(x: 0.25, y: -0.25, color: .green),
    Vertex(x: -0.25, y: -0.25, color: .red),
    Vertex(x: 0.0, y: 0.25, color: .blue)
]
```

But what are the clip space coordinates, and why do these coordinates render a triangle at the center of the screen?

This positioning is due to the clip-space coordinate system, which places the viewport's lower-left corner at $(-1.0, -1.0)$ and the upper-right corner at $(1.0, 1.0)$. Figure 4-1 and Figure 4-2 are representing this coordinate system in 2D.

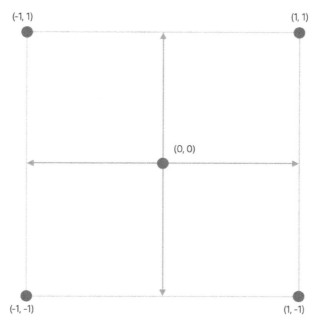

Figure 4-1. *2D representation of Metal coordinate system*

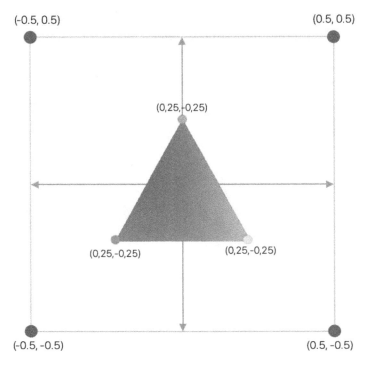

Figure 4-2. *Triangle vertices position on the 2D representation of the Metal coordinate system*

Figure 4-2 is a simplified version. Clip-space coordinates represent the 3D position as a 4D homogeneous vector. But because we're working in 2D only so far, the last two dimensions are static, and we won't explore them yet.

To practice coordinate transformation, you will update your vertex function to receive vertex coordinates in a viewport coordinate space.

To do so, the vertex function should receive one additional argument: viewportSize. Then, according to the viewport size, you calculate the result of the vertex position in metal coordinates. For example, if your viewportSize is (1400, 1600), your triangle vertices positions will be represented as shown in Figure 4-3.

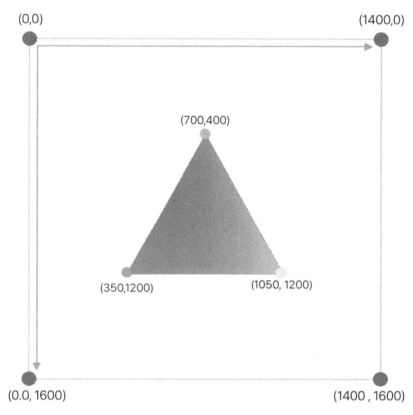

Figure 4-3. *Triangle vertices position according to viewport*

But before you begin the implementation of these updates, let's overview the changes made in the sample project.

The Starter Project

Open, build, and run the starter project from a folder named 04-shader-functions. Once your project is running, there are three menu items in the pre-implemented user interface shown in Figure 4-4.

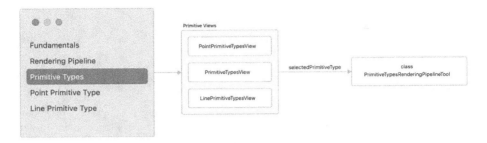

Figure 4-4. *A process of handling selected primitive type*

As you can see in this diagram, your starter project includes only one implementation of the RenderingTool protocol. However, it serves as a command encoder for multiple MetalViews.

In this example, you practice a different pipelineState configuration depending on the selectedPrimitiveType.

Transform Viewport Coordinates in a Vertex Function

To receive the viewportSize argument in the vertex function, you must first create new vertex and fragment functions. New functions are required because the older one is already used in the rendering pipeline example, and to keep it working after updates, you must create new shader functions.

Create a new file named PrimitiveTypesShader.metal and insert the following code.

```
struct Vertex {
    float4 position [[position]];
    float4 color;
};
```

```
vertex Vertex shaderViewportPositionedVertex(constant Vertex
*vertices [[ buffer(0) ]],
                        constant vector_uint2 *viewportSize
                        Pointer [[ buffer(1) ]],
                                        uint vid [[
vertex_id ]]) {
    Vertex in = vertices[vid];
    vector_float2 viewportSize = vector_float2(*viewport
    izePointer);

    Vertex out;
    float2 pos = float2(in.position.x, in.position.y);
    out.position = float4(pos, 0, 1);
    out.color = in.color;
    return out;
}
```

Open `PrimitiveTypesRenderingPipelineTool.swift` and replace the `shaderVertex` string with `shaderViewportPositionedVertex` in the `createPipelineStateIfNeeded` function.

After that, in the `handleRenderEncoder` function, insert this line before the `drawPrimitives` method.

```
// Pass the viewport size
var viewportSize = vector_uint2(viewportSize.width.int32,
viewportSize.height.int32)
encoder.setVertexBytes(&viewportSize, length:
(MemoryLayout<vector_uint2>.stride), index: 1)
```

After making these changes, build and run your project. The rendering result should be the same as in the starter project.

The next step after receiving the additional `viewportSize` argument is the transformation to clip space coordinates. To do so, insert the following code into the `shaderViewportPositionedVertex` vertex function.

```
float x = in.position.x;
float y = in.position.y;

float halfWidth = viewportSize.x / 2;
float targetX = (x / halfWidth) - 1.0;
if (x == halfWidth) {
    targetX = 0;
}

float halfHeight = viewportSize.y / 2;
float targetY = 1.0 - (y / halfHeight);
if (y == halfHeight) {
    targetY = 0;
}

Vertex out;
float2 pos = float2(targetX, targetY);
```

Afterward, the vertex function can calculate the vertex location relative to `viewportSize`, so let's update the vertices' data locations with the viewport-aligned one. Return to the `handleRenderEncoder` function and replace an old vertices array with the new one.

```
let vertices = [
    Vertex(x: viewportSize.width / 2, y: viewportSize.height
    / 2 - 150, color: .green),
    Vertex(x: viewportSize.width / 2 - 150, y: viewport
    Size.height / 2 + 150, color: .red),
    Vertex(x: viewportSize.width / 2 + 150, y: viewport
    Size.height / 2 + 150, color: .blue)
]
```

Build and run your project. You should get the same result as shown in Figure 4-5.

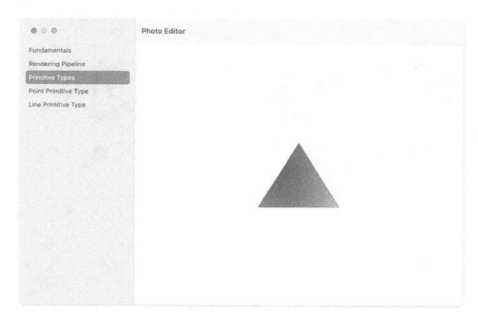

Figure 4-5. *The rendering result calculated relative to viewportSize*

The rendering result should be the same as before, but now the difference is that it's calculated relative to `viewportSize`.

However, getting the same result after so many updates is frustrating, so let's try some experiments.

Replace the vertices array with the following code.

```
let vertices = [ Vertex(x: 200, y: 100, color: .green),
Vertex(x: 50.0, y: 300, color: .red), Vertex(x: 250.0, y: 450,
color: .blue) ]
```

After that, your result should be different.

Once you implement the example, you'll be ready for a detailed overview of coordinate transformations in vertex functions.

Figure 4-6 outlines each step involved in vertex coordinate transformation.

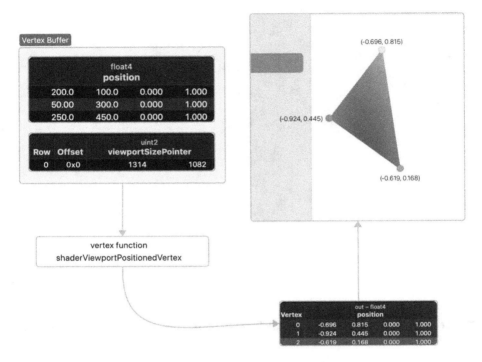

Figure 4-6. *Coordinate transformations in vertex functions*

The vertex shader function receives a vertex buffer containing three vertices with positions (200, 100), (50, 300), and (250, 450). It also receives vertex bytes containing `viewportSize` (1314, 1082).

After that, the vertex shader function is executed, and according to input data, it transforms the vertices' positions to clip-space coordinates. For instance, the following is a transformation of the first vertex's position.

`(200, 100): 200/(1314/2) - 1.0 = -0.696 (targetX); 1.0 - 100/ (1082/2) = 0.815 (targetY)`

As a result, the transformed Vertex is displayed in a layout that mirrors its appearance with UIKit, demonstrating the practical application of the transformation.

Coordinate Systems

The result of the vertex function returns a variable with an attribute [[position]] in a 4D coordinate system.

However, you described the position attribute with only two variables: x and y, because both models from the previous examples defined their z and w position's properties with a default value of 0 and 1, respectively.

For example, the following is the position from the shaderViewportPositionedVertex vertex function.

```
out.position = float4(pos, 0, 1);
```

And its z and w dimensions are static.

Understanding Coordinate Spaces

In Metal, different stages of the rendering pipeline use various coordinate spaces to process and render graphics. Coordinate spaces are important for working with graphics in Metal. They define how points in a space are located and represented on your device's screen.

Clip Space Coordinates

Clip space coordinates represent a 4D homogeneous coordinate system.

This system includes the (x, y, z, w) components, where w is used for **perspective division**, which transforms clip space coordinates into normalized device coordinates (NDC).

We're not going to focus on the perspective division right now.

For now, let's just remember that the position attribute of the result of a vertex function contains four components. After a vertex function, the rasterization stage returns a rendering result with a position in normalized device coordinates.

Normalized Device Coordinates

Normalized device coordinates (NDC) represent a stage in the rendering pipeline where coordinates are transformed to x, y, and z values ranging between –1.0 and 1.0. With that system, graphics are device-independent, allowing consistent rendering across different screen sizes and resolutions. Figure 4-7 illustrates the NDC system and its representation of the viewport. The NDC system positions the viewport's lower-left corner at $(−1.0, −1.0)$ and the upper-right corner at $(1.0, 1.0)$, with positive z values extending into the screen, defining the depth.

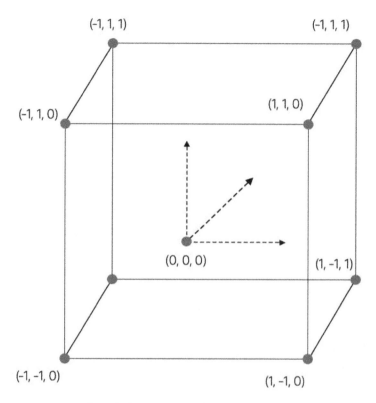

Figure 4-7. *Normalized device coordinates*

Viewport Coordinates

After processing through the NDC stage, coordinates are transformed into viewport coordinates by the rasterizer stage. This system maps NDC to specific pixel locations on the screen, with the origin at the top-left corner, as shown in Figure 4-8. Viewport coordinates are responsible for defining the actual size and position of objects as they appear on the display.

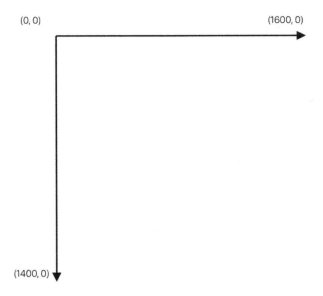

Figure 4-8. *Viewport coordinates*

During the rasterization stage, the vertex is positioned within various coordinate systems, finishing as dots positioned on a screen. After that, these dots are interpreted as specific geometric primitives during the next stage of the rendering pipeline— **primitive assembly**.

Primitive Assembly

So far you were introduced to the position transformation inside the vertex function, the result of which contained a transformed [[position]] attribute. Then, the rasterization stage transforms the position to a normalized device coordinate. After that, this set of vertices is interpreted into a primitive shape during the primitive assembly process. Figure 4-9 represents how a triangle is assembled from transformed vertices.

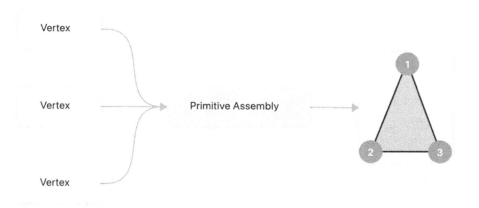

Figure 4-9. *Representation of the Primitive Assembly*

As you can see in the diagram, the `.triangle` is built from the three different vertices after their position transformations are finished.

So far, you worked only with triangles. It's time to explore all of the available primitives.

Primitive Types

`MTLRenderCommandEncoder` supports five geometric primitive types in the `drawPrimitives` command. To better understand these options, Figure 4-10 overviews the different primitive types available.

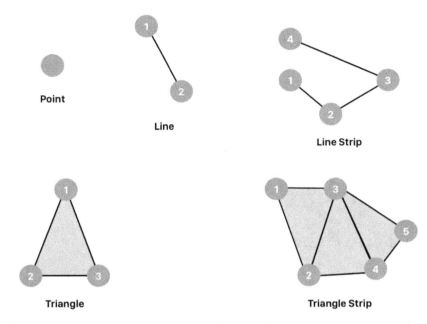

Figure 4-10. *Overview of geometric primitive types supported by Metal*

MTLPrimitiveType

- .point rasterizes a point at each vertex. The vertex shader must provide [[point_size]], or the point size is undefined.

- .line rasterizes a line between each pair of vertices, resulting in a series of unconnected lines. The last vertex is ignored if there are an odd number of vertices.

- .lineStrip rasterizes a line between each pair of adjacent vertices, resulting in a series of connected lines (also called a polyline).

- `.triangle` rasterizes a triangle for every separate set of three vertices. If the number of vertices is not a multiple of three, either one or two vertices is ignored.

- `.triangleStrip` rasterizes a triangle for every three adjacent vertices.

Draw Primitives

You're now familiar with the `drawPrimitives` GPU command. It initiates the rendering process with the selected type of primitive assembly.

Rendering a Line

Let's begin your journey with the primitive assembly by rendering a line instead of triangle.

1. Create a `drawPrimitives` command to support the selected type in the user interface. To do so, you must change the `drawPrimitives` call in `handleRenderEncoder` with the class argument updated by the user interface.

   ```
   encoder.drawPrimitives(type: selectedPrimitiveType,
   vertexStart: .zero, vertexCount: vertices.count)
   ```

2. Change the data encoded to a buffer with the correct amount according to `selectedPrimitiveType`.

   ```
   let vertices: [Vertex]

   switch selectedPrimitiveType {
   case .line:
       vertices = [
   ```

```
        Vertex(x: viewportSize.width / 2 - 150,
        y: viewportSize.height / 2, color: .red),
        Vertex(x: viewportSize.width / 2 + 150,
        y: viewportSize.height / 2, color: .blue)
    ]
case .point:
    vertices = [Vertex(x: viewportSize.width / 2, y:
    viewport
    Size.height / 2, color: .red)]
default:
    vertices = [
        Vertex(x: viewportSize.width / 2, y: viewport
        Size.height / 2 - 150, color: .green),
        Vertex(x: viewportSize.width / 2 - 150, y:
        viewport
        Size.height / 2 + 150, color: .red),
        Vertex(x: viewportSize.width / 2 + 150, y:
        viewport
        Size.height / 2 + 150, color: .blue)
    ]
}
```

As you can see, a switch case was made not only
for the .line primitive type, but for .point as well.
This was done to prevent a critical exception
when PointPrimitiveView is selected in the user
interface.

3.   Build and run your project.

Figure 4-11 demonstrates the result of the .line primitive rendered
from the viewportSize.width / 2 - 150 coordinates to viewportSize.
width / 2 + 150.

Figure 4-11. *Rendering result of a line primitive*

The `.lineStrip` is the same primitive type with only one difference: it has more than two vertices in the input with a line across each vertex.

It's the same with the `.triangleStrip` primitive type. It rasterizes a new triangle for every three vertices.

Point

The first difference between `.point` and other primitive types is the `[[point_size]]` vertex attribute, which is only available for the `.point` vertex function.

The implementation of a point begins with a new vertex shader and fragment functions. You need an additional vertex function to return a different vertex type, which is extended by a property with a `[[point_size]]` attribute.

But before implementing vertex and fragment functions for the `.point` primitive type, let's do a little refactoring and create a couple of functions to convert a viewport position to the clip space coordinates. To make a function visible in the Metal shader file for other functions, you must first declare these functions by inserting these lines.

```
using namespace metal;
//...
float xPositionInViewport(float x, vector_float2 viewportSize);
float yPositionInViewport(float y, vector_float2 viewportSize);
//...
// vertex ...
```

After the functions are declared, they become visible to other functions in this shader file. Now, the implementation.

```
float xPositionInViewport(float x, vector_float2
viewportSize) {
    float halfWidth = viewportSize.x / 2;
    float targetX = (x / halfWidth) - 1.0;
    if (x == halfWidth) {
        targetX = 0;
    }
    return targetX;
}

float yPositionInViewport(float y, vector_float2 viewportSize) {
    float halfHeight = viewportSize.y / 2;
    float targetY = 1.0 - (y / halfHeight);
    if (y == halfHeight) {
        targetY = 0;
    }
    return targetY;
}
```

After creating the xPositionInViewport and yPositionInViewport functions, you need to update the old viewport transformation code by replacing all the calculations with these two executions.

```
out.position = float4(xPositionInViewport(in.position.x,
            viewportSize),
                yPositionInViewport(in.position.y,
                viewportSize), 0, 1);
```

After that, you can continue the point vertex function implementation without repeating your old code. Here is the complete vertex function source code.

```
struct PointVertex {
    float4 position [[position]];
    float4 color;
    float size [[point_size]];
};
vertex PointVertex pointShaderViewportPositionedVertex(constant
Vertex *vertices [[ buffer(0) ]],
                        constant vector_uint2 *viewportSize
                        Pointer [[ buffer(1) ]],
                        uint vid [[ vertex_id ]]) {
    Vertex in = vertices[vid];
    vector_float2 viewportSize = vector_float2(*viewport
    SizePointer);

    PointVertex out;
    out.position = float4(xPositionInViewport(in.position.x,
                    viewportSize),
                    yPositionInViewport(in.position.y,
                    viewportSize), 0, 1);
    out.color = in.color;
```

```
    out.size = 20;
    return out;
};
```

And the last update in the shader file is to delete fragment creation.

```
fragment half4 pointShaderFragment(PointVertex point_data [[
stage_in ]],
                          float2 pointCoord  [[ point_coord ]])
{
    float dist = length(pointCoord - float2(0.5));
    float4 out_color = point_data.color;
    out_color.a = 1.0 - smoothstep(0.4, 0.5, dist);
    return half4(out_color);
};
```

In the implementation, the pointShaderFragment function calculates the distance between the point coordinate and the center of the point being drawn. Based on this distance, it returns either a transparent color (resulting in a circular point shape) or the point color specified in the PointVertex structure.

Now, when the point primitive has all the required shader functions to render, you only need to update PrimitiveTypesRenderingPipelineTool for the correct processing of the new shader functions. The first obvious change is the injection of different types of shader functions according to the selected primitive type.

```
 let vertexFunction = defaultLibrary?.
makeFunction(name: selectedPrimitiveType ==
.point ? "pointShaderViewportPositionedVertex" :
"shaderViewportPositionedVertex")
let fragmentFunction = defaultLibrary?.makeFunction(name:
selectedPrimitiveType == .point ? "pointShaderFragment" :
"shaderFragment")
```

Let's build the sample project and verify the result (see Figure 4-12).

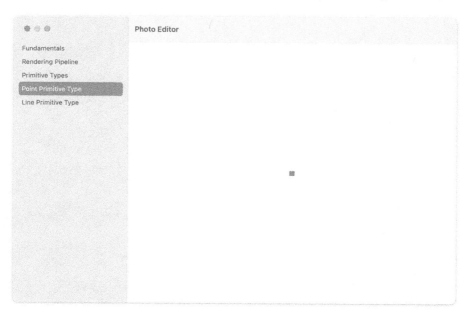

Figure 4-12. *The result of rendering a point primitive*

The result is not as expected: the point isn't rounded. Why? It happened because the fragment shader function returns an alpha value depending on the distance from the center to the border. But this alpha color doesn't render with transparency.

To fix this issue, you must update `pipelineDescriptor` to make the alpha transparent and enable blending.

```
if selectedPrimitiveType == .point {
    pipelineDescriptor.colorAttachments[0].
isBlendingEnabled = true
    pipelineDescriptor.colorAttachments[0].destinationRGBBl
    endFactor = .oneMinusSourceAlpha
}
```

With these changes, you can see a perfectly rounded point, as shown in Figure 4-13.

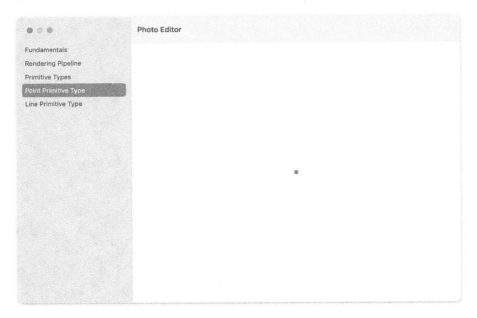

Figure 4-13. *Rounded point achieved through alpha blending*

Conclusion

In this chapter, you learned about the vertex function, including

- Supported attributes for the vertex function return type.

- Typical transformations performed in a vertex function and how to translate viewport coordinates to Metal's coordinate system.

- A basic introduction to different coordinate spaces.

- The process of interpreting vertex positions into a geometrical shape (primitive type).

- The kinds of primitive types supported in Metal

CHAPTER 5

Transformations

In the previous chapter, you learned about different coordinate systems used in Metal. This chapter teaches you how to translate, scale, and rotate objects around the screen.

The Starter Project

1. Open and run the starter project.

   The starter project includes the following.

   - The **SwiftUI Interface**, illustrated in Figure 5-1, updates the transformation parameters of the object. Sliders are connected to the @Published values inside CoordinateSpaceRenderingTool.

   - CoordinateSpaceRenderingTool, an implementation of the RenderingTool protocol.

© Bogdan Redkin and Victor Yaskevich 2024
B. Redkin and V. Yaskevich, *Master Photo and Video Editing with Metal*,
https://doi.org/10.1007/979-8-8688-0832-6_5

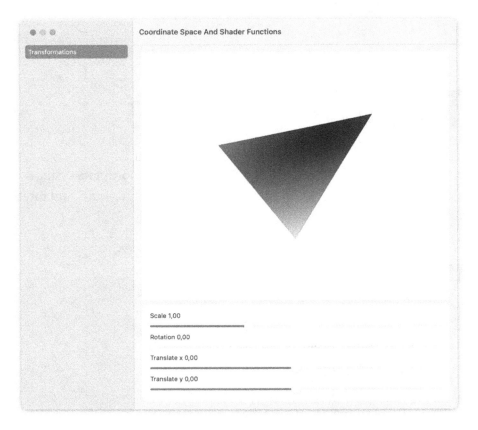

Figure 5-1. *The initial interface includes transformation controls*

CoordinateSpaceRenderingTool renders a triangle with three vertices, described as follows.

```
let vertices: [Vertex] = [
    Vertex(position: [-0.5, 0.25, 0.0, 1.0], color:
    [1, 0, 0, 1]),  // Bottom Left
    Vertex(position: [0.0, -0.5, 0.0, 1.0], color:
    [0, 1, 0, 1]), // Bottom Right
    Vertex(position: [0.5, 0.5, 0.0, 1.0], color:
    [0, 0, 1, 1])    // Top
]
```

72

Let's look at the vertex positions; they are described in a normalized device coordinate system (NDC).

You learned in the previous chapter that vertex [[position]] attribute qualifier is always in the **clip space coordinate system**. But since the perspective transformations are not used, the w dimension is set to default 1.

And if w is 1, clip space coordinates are always equal to normalized device coordinates.

Figures 5-2 and 5-3 are visual representations of the triangle's vertex positions, which you're going to translate by a vector (–0.4, 0.4).

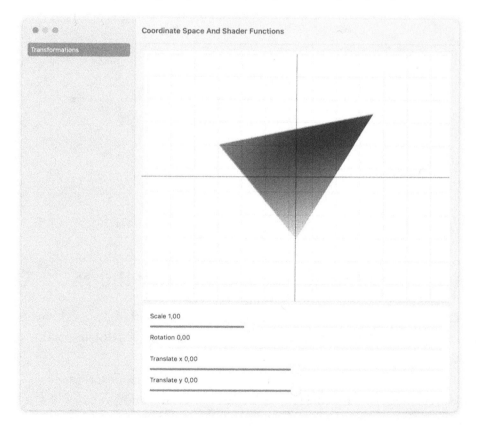

Figure 5-2. *The rendered triangle result with grid overlay*

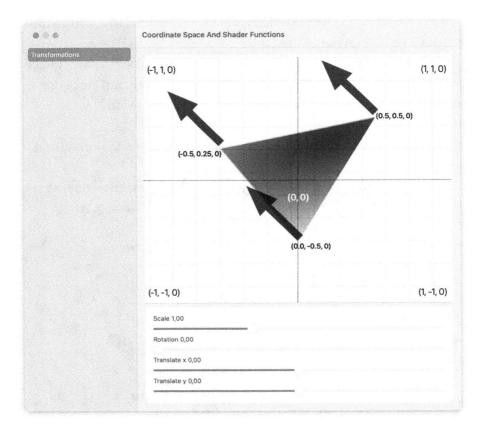

Figure 5-3. *Arrows represent translation by (–0.4, 0.4)*

Add a Vector to the Vertex Coordinate

Figure 5-2 shows the initial position of the rendered triangle. A grid overlay is applied to visualize the effect of translation. Figure 5-3 illustrates the translation by the vector (–0.4, 0.4).

What is a **vector**? It's a structure of coordinates that describe displacement in a space. Figure 5-3 features a translation vector (–0.4, 0.4), which means that each vertex position is changed by –0.4 at x and 0.4 at y.

Open the CoordinateSpaceRenderingTool.swift and add a new class variable named time. This variable performs smooth animation from the current vertex position to translation. You also need to update the handleRenderEncoder method to calculate a new translationVector.

```
var time: Float = 0

func handleRenderEncoder(encoder: MTLRenderCommandEncoder,
metalView mtkView: MTKView, viewportSize: CGSize) {
    createPipelineStateIfNeeded(metalView: mtkView)

    guard let pipelineState = self.pipelineState else {
    return }
    encoder.setRenderPipelineState(pipelineState)

    time += 0.005
    let currentTime = sin(time)
    var percentage: Float
    if currentTime < 0 {
        percentage = currentTime / -1.0
    } else if currentTime > 0 {
        percentage = currentTime / 1.0
    } else {
        percentage = 0.5
    }
    let translationVector = simd_float3(-0.4 * percentage, 0.4
    * percentage, 0)
    // Define triangle vertices
    let vertices: [Vertex] = [
        Vertex(position: [-0.5, 0.25, 0.0, 1.0] + simd_float4
        (translationVector, 0.0), color: [1, 0, 0, 1]),
        // Bottom Left
```

```
Vertex(position: [0.0, -0.5, 0.0, 1.0] + simd_
float4(translationVector, 0.0), color: [0, 1, 0, 1]),
// Bottom Right
Vertex(position: [0.5, 0.5, 0.0, 1.0] + simd_float4
(translationVector, 0.0), color: [0, 0, 1, 1])    // Top
]
```

The code does the following three things (also see Figures 5-4, 5-5, and 5-6).

- It calculates the current percentage of the translation transform. For each frame, increase the time variable and then extract a sine value from the time. The result of the sine calculation is always between –1 and 1, so no matter how many increments of time there are, you can always calculate the exact percentage of translation progress.

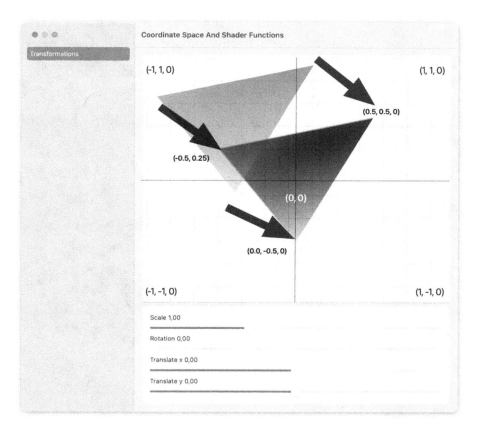

Figure 5-4. *Translation vertex position by applying vector re, the object moves from (0.0, –0.5) to (–0.4, –0.1))*

- It generates a new `translationVector` based on the current translation from the percentage.

- It applies the translation transformation vector to the current vertex position coordinate.

With these updates, the triangle vertex starts smoothly moving to the destination coordinates and backward to the center.

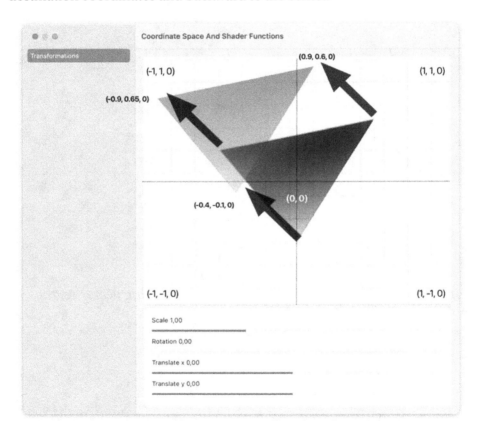

Figure 5-5. *Translation vertex position. By applying vector (–0.4, –0.1), the object moves from (0.0, –0.5) to (–0.4, –0.1), from (0.5, 0.5) to (0.9, 0.6)*

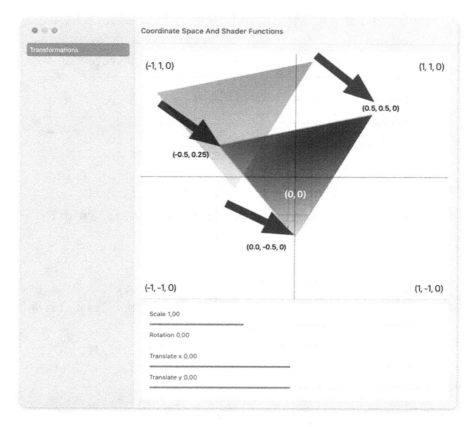

Figure 5-6. *Translation vertex position. By reversing the previous transformation result, the object moves from (0.0, –0.5) to (–0.4, –0.1)*

Before proceeding to the next step, updating the transformation parameters by sliders, you must remove the previously added code related to the translationVector.

So, delete your time class variable and then clean the handleRenderEncoder method.

```
func handleRenderEncoder(encoder: MTLRenderCommandEncoder,
metalView mtkView: MTKView, viewportSize: CGSize) {
    createPipelineStateIfNeeded(metalView: mtkView)
```

```
guard let pipelineState = self.pipelineState else {
return }
encoder.setRenderPipelineState(pipelineState)

// Define triangle vertices
let vertices: [Vertex] = [
    Vertex(position: [-0.5, 0.25, 0.0, 1.0], color:
    [1, 0, 0, 1]),  // Bottom Left
    Vertex(position: [0.0, -0.5, 0.0, 1.0], color:
    [0, 1, 0, 1]), // Bottom Right
    Vertex(position: [0.5, 0.5, 0.0, 1.0], color:
    [0, 0, 1, 1])    // Top
]

let vertexBuffer = device.makeBuffer(bytes: vertices,
length: vertices.count * MemoryLayout<Vertex>.stride,
options: .storageModeShared)
encoder.setVertexBuffer(vertexBuffer, offset: 0,
index: 0)

encoder.drawPrimitives(type: .triangle, vertexStart: 0,
vertexCount: vertices.count)
}
```

You already should have a basic understanding of how the vertex's position could be transformed.

Now, let's proceed to the vertex transformation to any shape and size with the power of using matrixes.

The first step is to handle a new value when any of the sliders have been updated.

Slider Updates

1. Open `CoordinateSpaceRenderingTool.swift`
   and insert a new class variable right after the
   `pipelineState` variable declaration.

   ```
   private var transformBindings: AnyCancellable?
   ```

2. Update the `deinit` method in
   `CoordinateSpaceRenderingTool` with the
   cancelation of unnecessary bindings

   ```
   deinit {
       transformBindings?.cancel()
       transformBindings = nil
   }
   ```

3. Update the `setupBindings` method by adding a
   subscription to the transform parameters updates.

   ```
   private func setupBindings() {
       transformBindings = $rotationTransform
           .combineLatest($translateTransformX, $translate
           TransformY, $scaleTransform)
           .filter({
               $0.0 != self.rotationTransform ||
       $0.1 != self.translateTransformX ||
       $0.2 != self.translateTransformY ||
       $0.3 != self.scaleTransform
   })
   ```

```
.receive(on: DispatchQueue.main)
.sink { [weak self] rotation, translationX,
translationY, scale in

    guard let self else { return }

    print("rotation: \(rotation) translation
    \(translationX),\(translationY), scale \(scale)")
}
}
```

Transformation Matrixes

A transformation matrix is a mathematical tool that modifies the coordinates of points in space, effectively changing the position, orientation, or size of objects.

A matrix is a 4x4 array of numbers arranged in rows and columns, which can be used to represent a set of equations that describe transformations.

If you're familiar with the **CATransform3D** matrix, the transformations in Metal wouldn't be a problem since the transformation matrix in Metal has the same transform parameter mapping. For example, the equation shown in Figure 5-7 demonstrates the identity transformation matrix.

$$\begin{bmatrix} 1 & 0 & 0 & 0 \\ 0 & 1 & 0 & 0 \\ 0 & 0 & 1 & 0 \\ 0 & 0 & 0 & 1 \end{bmatrix}$$

Figure 5-7. *Identity transformation matrix*

Matrix Implementation

Let's continue matrix implementation by adding the next two
transformations: scale (see Figure 5-8) and translate (see Figure 5-9).

$$\begin{bmatrix} s_x & 0 & 0 & 0 \\ 0 & s_y & 0 & 0 \\ 0 & 0 & s_z & 0 \\ 0 & 0 & 0 & 1 \end{bmatrix}$$

Figure 5-8. *Scale transformation matrix*

$$\begin{bmatrix} 1 & 0 & 0 & 0 \\ 0 & 1 & 0 & 0 \\ 0 & 0 & 1 & 0 \\ t_x & t_y & t_z & 1 \end{bmatrix}$$

Figure 5-9. *Translate transformation matrix*

1. Open the `Matrix + Transformations.swift` file
   and define custom matrix initializers with the
   following code.

```
init(translation t: simd_float3) {
    self.init([1, 0, 0, 0],
              [0, 1, 0, 0],
              [0, 0, 1, 0],
              [t.x, t.y, t.z, 1])
}
```

```
init(scale s: CGPoint) {
    self.init([s.x.float, 0, 0, 0],
              [0, s.y.float, 0, 0],
              [0, 0, 1, 0],
              [0, 0, 0, 1])
}

init(rotation r: simd_float3) {
    let xRotationMatrix = matrix_float4x4(
                              [1, 0, 0, 0],
                              [0, r.x.cos,
                              r.x.sin, 0],
                              [0, -r.x.sin,
                              r.x.cos, 0],
                              [0, 0, 0, 1])

    let yRotationMatrix = matrix_float4x4(
[r.y.cos, 0, -r.y.sin, 0],
                              [0, 1, 0, 0],
                              [r.y.sin, 0,
                              r.y.cos, 0],
                              [0, 0, 0, 1])

    let zRotationMatrix = matrix_float4x4(
[r.z.cos, r.z.sin, 0, 0], [-r.z.sin, r.z.cos, 0, 0],
                              [0, 0, 1, 0],
                              [0, 0, 0, 1])

    self = xRotationMatrix * yRotationMatrix *
    zRotationMatrix
}
```

The following code describes `matrix_float4x4` initialized with scale, translation, or rotation transform.

As you can see, initialization with **rotation transform** is different from the two others; let's examine matrix representations in Figures 5-10, 5-11, and 5-12.

$$\begin{bmatrix} \cos(y) & 0 & -\sin(y) & 0 \\ 0 & 1 & 0 & 0 \\ \sin(y) & 0 & \cos(y) & 0 \\ 0 & 0 & 0 & 1 \end{bmatrix}$$

Figure 5-10. *Rotate around the y axis*

$$\begin{bmatrix} \cos(z) & \sin(z) & 0 & 0 \\ -\sin(z) & \cos(z) & 0 & 0 \\ 0 & 0 & 1 & 0 \\ 0 & 0 & 0 & 1 \end{bmatrix}$$

Figure 5-11. *Rotate around the z axis*

$$\begin{bmatrix} 1 & 0 & 0 & 0 \\ 0 & \cos(x) & \sin(x) & 0 \\ 0 & -\sin(x) & \cos(x) & 0 \\ 0 & 0 & 0 & 1 \end{bmatrix}$$

Figure 5-12. *Rotate around the x axis*

That is different because rotation transformation requires three different matrixes to describe transformations.

There is another great advantage of using matrixes instead of vectors: you can combine any transformation matrix with the simple multiplication of one matrix to another.

Matrix Multiplication

Matrix multiplication combines multiple transformations—translation, scaling, and rotation—into one seamless operation.

In the context of transformation matrixes, multiplication is not commutative; the order of multiplication matters. This means that rotating an object and then translating it returns a different result than translating first and then rotating.

How to Multiply Matrixes

For two matrixes, *A* and *B*, to be multiplied, the number of columns in *A* must match the number of rows in *B*. Since both example matrixes are 3x3, they meet this requirement perfectly.

Step-by-Step Matrix Multiplication

To multiply matrix A by matrix B and obtain matrix $C = AB$, follow these steps for each element in C, where i is the row index and j is the column index.

1. Select row i from A.

2. Select column j from B.

3. Multiply the corresponding elements and sum them up to get the element c(ij).

Example

Consider two 3x3 matrixes, A and B, defined as illustrated in Figure 5-13.

$$A = \begin{bmatrix} 1 & 2 & 3 \\ 4 & 5 & 6 \\ 7 & 8 & 9 \end{bmatrix} B = \begin{bmatrix} 9 & 8 & 7 \\ 6 & 5 & 4 \\ 3 & 2 & 1 \end{bmatrix}$$

Figure 5-13. *Matrix multiplication example*

To calculate $C = AB$, you'll find one of the elements as an example, specifically c(23) (row 2, column 3 of C).

1. Take row 2 from A: 4, 5, 6.

2. Take column 3 from B: 7, 4, 1.

3. Multiply them pairwise and sum: 4 * 7 + 5 * 4 + 6 * 1 = 28 + 20 + 6 = 54.

Thus, the element at the second row and third column of C is 54.

Multiplication Results

Performing these steps for each element of the resulting matrix C, you get a complex equation, as shown in Figure 5-14.

$$C = AB = \begin{bmatrix} (1*9+2*6+3*3) & (1*8+2*5+3*2) & (1*7+2*4+3*1) \\ (4*9+5*6+6*3) & (4*8+5*5+6*2) & (4*7+5*4+6*1) \\ (7*9+8*6+9*3) & (7*8+8*5+9*2) & (7*7+8*4+9*1) \end{bmatrix}$$

Figure 5-14. *Matrix multiplication equation*

The result of this multiplication is shown in Figure 5-15.

$$C = \begin{bmatrix} 30 & 24 & 18 \\ 84 & 69 & 54 \\ 138 & 114 & 90 \end{bmatrix}$$

Figure 5-15. *Matrix multiplication result*

Applying Matrix Transformations in Shaders

And the first step is generation transformation matrixes with updated values from sliders.

Create class variables in CoordinateSpaceRenderingTool.swift to store the matrixes result.

```
private var translateTransformationMatrix: matrix_float4x4
private var rotationTransformationMatrix: matrix_float4x4
private var scaleTransformationMatrix: matrix_float4x4
private var transformationMatrix: matrix_float4x4
```

Paste the following code with default matrixes initialization at the end of init implementation.

```
//default transformation paramaters set-up
//...
self.translateTransformationMatrix = matrix_
float4x4(translation: .zero)
self.rotationTransformationMatrix = matrix_
float4x4(rotation: .zero)
self.scaleTransformationMatrix = matrix_float4x4(scale:
CGPoint(x: 1.0, y: 1.0))
self.transformationMatrix = self.translateTransformationMatrix
* self.rotationTransformationMatrix * self.
scaleTransformationMatrix
```

Then, you need to update transformBindings subscription handler.

```
//setupBindings -> transformBindings...
.sink { [weak self] rotation, translationX, translationY, scale
in guard let self else { return }

    print("rotation: \(rotation) translation \(translationX),
    \(translationY), scale \(scale)")

    self.translateTransformationMatrix = .init(translation:
    .init(translationX, translationY, .zero))
    self.rotationTransformationMatrix = .init(rotation:
    .init(0.0, 0.0, rotation.cgFloat.degreesToRadians().float))
    self.scaleTransformationMatrix = .init(scale: .init(x:
    scale.cgFloat, y: scale.cgFloat))
    self.transformationMatrix = self.translateTransformation
    Matrix * self.rotationTransformationMatrix * self.scale
    TransformationMatrix
}
```

Now, when you can generate `transformationMatrix` with values from sliders, you have only one step left: updating the vertex function with vertex position transformation by `transformationMatrix`. Open `CoordinateSpaceShader.metal` and update `matrixTransformVertexShader` with the following code.

```
vertex VertexOut matrixTransformVertexShader(const device
VertexIn *vertices [[buffer(0)]],

                                    constant float4x4
                                    &transformMatrix
                                    [[buffer(1)]],
                                    uint vid
[[vertex_id]]) {
    VertexOut outVertex;
    VertexIn inVertex = vertices[vid];

    outVertex.position = transformMatrix * inVertex.position;
    outVertex.color = inVertex.color;

    return outVertex;
}
```

With updates from the following code, now your `matrixTransformVertexShader` can receive `transformMatrix` as a buffer input argument with index = 1. Received `transformMatrix` argument then used to transform the position of `outVertex`.

After the `outVertex` position is multiplied with `transformMatrix` values, `outVertex` is transformed according to the `transformMatrix` scale, rotation, and translation.

Now, you need to pass `transformMatrix` as an argument to the vertex function. To do so, go to `CoordinateSpaceRenderingTool.swift` and add the following to the `handleRenderEncoder` function before `encoder.drawPrimitives` is called.

```
encoder.setVertexBytes(&transformationMatrix,
                        length: MemoryLayout<matrix_
                               float4x4>.stride,
                        index: 1)
```

Build and run your project. As demonstrated in Figures 5-16 and 5-17, you should be able to transform the triangle vertex with new slider values in the final result.

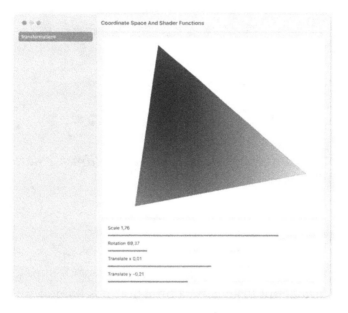

Figure 5-16. *Triangle positions after applying combined translation, rotation, and scaling transformations*

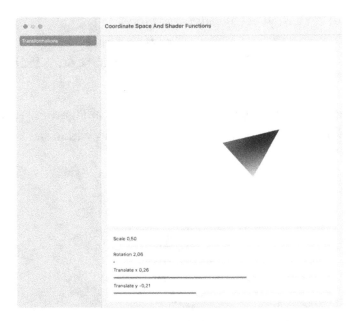

Figure 5-17. *Triangle positions after scaling transformation changed to 0,5*

Conclusion

In this chapter, you gain an understanding of the techniques for managing object transformations to achieve control over positioning, orientation and scaling with matrix multiplication. Here is a list of major key points covered in this chapter:

- **Normalized device coordinates** provide a standardized way to define object positions, making them independent of the viewport size for consistent rendering across different display dimensions.

- **Vectors** are used to describe the displacement in space by specifying directional movement along the X and Y axes.

- **Transformation matrixes** efficiently represent complex transformations, allowing for modifying objects' positions, orientations, sizes, and perspectives.

- **Matrix multiplication** allows the combination of multiple transformations into one operation. The order of multiplication matters.

- **Shader implementation** demonstrates how transformation matrixes are applied dynamically in metal shaders to transform vertex positions.

CHAPTER 6

Perspective Transformations

Previous chapters introduced the homogeneous coordinate system, explored how the objects are represented differently based on their distance from the viewer's perspective, and guided you through implementing transformation matrices to manipulate vertex coordinates in 2D.

This chapter combines this knowledge with more complex matrices and can make perspective projection transformations of the vertex coordinates in 3D.

Clip Space Coordinates

Clip space coordinates represent a 4D homogeneous coordinate system.

This system includes the (x, y, z, w) components, where w is used for **perspective division**, which transforms clip space coordinates into normalized device coordinates (NDC).

The following code is from the previous chapter. Recall that the `[[position]]` attribute qualifier has the `float4` data type.

© Bogdan Redkin and Victor Yaskevich 2024
B. Redkin and V. Yaskevich, *Master Photo and Video Editing with Metal*,
https://doi.org/10.1007/979-8-8688-0832-6_6

```
struct Vertex {
    float4 position [[position]];
    float4 color;
};
```

What Is the w Dimension?

The w dimension is the distance from the point of view to the object. w is 1 by default, which means no scale at all. All clip-space coordinates are converted to the normalized device coordinates equally. Figure 6-1 shows the basic structure of the clip-space coordinate system, and Figure 6-2 demonstrates this division process with the default scale in action.

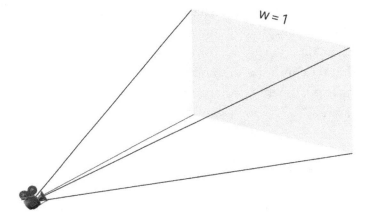

Figure 6-1. *w dimension in 4D homogeneous coordinates*

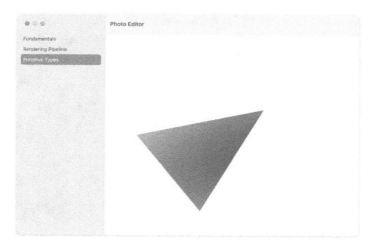

Figure 6-2. *The default scale of perspective division*

The rasterizer divides the x, y, and z values by w to convert clip-space coordinates into normalized device coordinates. It's called **perspective division**.

Figure 6-3 shows the equality defines the conversion from the clip space coordinates (c) to the normalized device coordinates (n).

$$\begin{pmatrix} x_n \\ y_n \\ z_n \end{pmatrix} = \begin{pmatrix} x_c/w_c \\ y_c/w_c \\ z_c/w_c \end{pmatrix}$$

Figure 6-3. *Mathematical conversion from the clip-space coordinates to the normalized device coordinates*

Let's look at a few examples of perspective division.

Figures 6-4, 6-5, and 6-6 illustrate scenarios where w is set to 3, which means that the point of view is further from the rendering object.

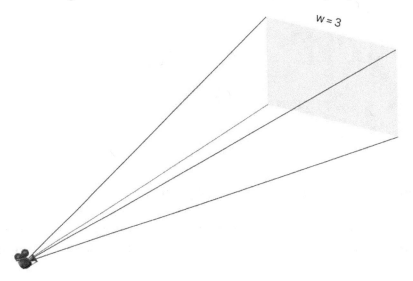

Figure 6-4. *Illustration of perspective division with w = 3 in clip-space coordinate system*

Figure 6-5. *The rendering result of the triangle from the previous example, all the coordinates are the same, but* w *is 3*

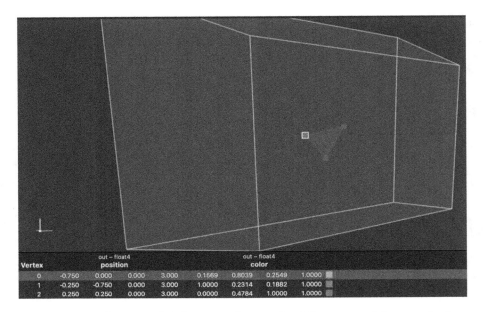

Vertex	out – float4 position				out – float4 color				
0	-0.750	0.000	0.000	3.000	0.1569	0.8039	0.2549	1.0000	
1	-0.250	-0.750	0.000	3.000	1.0000	0.2314	0.1882	1.0000	
2	0.250	0.250	0.000	3.000	0.0000	0.4784	1.0000	1.0000	

Figure 6-6. *The Metal debugger shows the 3D space of the rendering scene, and the triangle is further than it was where the w was 1*

Figure 6-7 illustrates the w set to 0.5, so the point of view is closer to the rendering object.

Figure 6-7. *The rendering result of the triangle, which is scaled by the perspective division 0, 5*

So, the **perspective division converts the vertex clip space position** to the normalized device coordinates.

Introduction to Projection Perspective

Let's start with the introduction to the projective geometry. You discovered the w dimension and how it affects the rendering result in terms of scale.

But what if objects needed scaling not solely by distance but also from varied viewpoints like the human eye sees the world? Figure 6-8 shows the perspective frustum used in calculating the projection transformation matrix.

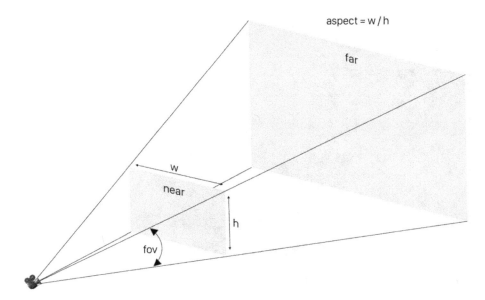

Figure 6-8. *Perspective frustum*

Figure 6-8 illustrates the **projection transformation matrix** and the variables used in the calculation.

- **Field of view (fovY)** is an angle of view represented as the cotangent of half of the field of view angle.

- **Aspect** is the aspect ratio of the viewport.

- **Near** and **far** are variables working together to get the ratio between the closest and the most distant objects so you can calculate the actual perspective.

Understanding the Math

The perspective projection matrix comprises several components, each responsible for different aspects of the transformation. The matrix breakdown is illustrated in Figure 6-9.

$$fovY = \left\{ \frac{\pi \times fovDegree}{180} \right\}(1)$$
$$fovY \downarrow$$
$$f = \left\{ \frac{1}{tan(\frac{fovY}{2})} \right\}(2)$$
$$\left.(3)^2 \right\} \Rightarrow f$$

$$\begin{bmatrix} \frac{f}{aspect} & 0 & 0 & 0 \\ 0 & f & 0 & 0 \\ 0 & \frac{far}{far - near} & -near * \frac{far}{far - near} & 0 \\ 0 & 0 & 1 & 0 \end{bmatrix}$$

Figure 6-9. *Components of the perspective projection matrix*

Let's explore each component in this matrix.

- **First row**: Responsible for the X scaling. This dimension is based on the aspect ratio and field of view, so a narrower field of view or a wider aspect ratio makes objects appear wider.

- **Second row**: It is the scaling of a Y dimension, and since the angle of the field of view is based only on the Y dimension, you can use it straightforwardly as the Y scale parameter. As a result, the narrower the field of view is, the taller the object appears.

- **Third row**: Adjusts the Z component for depth perception, including which parts of the scene are visible within the near and far clipping panes.

- **Fourth row**: Brings in the projective aspect, transforming coordinates to enable perspective division and adjusting the W coordinates scale based on depth.

But before going any further, let's prepare a subject for your transformations. It's time to move from a triangle to a rectangle since it's a more visual form for demonstration.

Draw a Rectangle

Open the starter project. Since the previous chapter, it has had a few updates. Besides the UI Interface required for these transformations, there is also a new implementation of the `RenderingTool` protocol: `ProjectionTransformationRenderingTool`.

Build and run your project.

Figure 6-10 shows the same triangle as in the previous chapter, and triangles are the core of our future photo editor application.

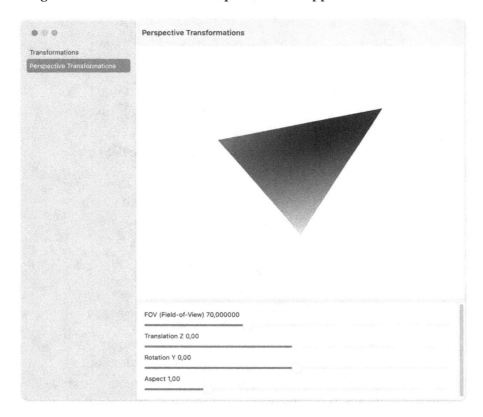

Figure 6-10. *The triangle from Chapter 5*

All photo editors are just variations of the 2D scene, and all of the images, layers, and any editable material here is a rectangle.

So, let's make one. During this chapter, the rectangle, because of its shape, will help you better understand how the transformation works.

1. But why is the .triangle primitive type used for that purpose? Is it the most efficient way to render rectangles in a 2D scene? Why not use the .point primitive type?

    You can't use the .point primitive type with the adjusted [[point_size]] attribute to map colors or a texture because it doesn't map to anything. You can see this in the triangle in Figure 6-10. It interpolates the color of each of the vertices and generates a gradient.

    And at this moment it's pretty clear that the .triangle primitive type is the best way to render rectangles because you just have to combine two triangles.

2. Open the ProjectionTransformationRenderingTool. swift and replace the vertices array describing a triangle with the one describing a rectangle.

```
let vertices: [Vertex] = [
    Vertex(position: [-0.5, -0.5, 0.0, 1.0], color:
    [1, 0, 0, 1]), //bottom left
    Vertex(position: [0.5, -0.5, 0.0, 1.0], color:
    [0, 1, 0, 1]), //bottom right
    Vertex(position: [-0.5, 0.5, 0.0, 1.0], color:
    [0, 0, 1, 1]), //top left
    Vertex(position: [-0.5, 0.5, 0.0, 1.0], color:
    [0, 0, 1, 1]), //top left
```

```
    Vertex(position: [0.5, 0.5, 0.0, 1.0], color:
    [0, 1, 0, 1]), //top right
    Vertex(position: [0.5, -0.5, 0.0, 1.0], color:
    [0, 1, 0, 1]) //bottom left
]
```

The code describes six vertices. Because of the
.triangle primitive type, these six points map into
two triangles.

3.   Build and run your project.

Figure 6-11 shows the Metal View debugger displaying six points
representing the vertices of two triangles forming a rectangle.

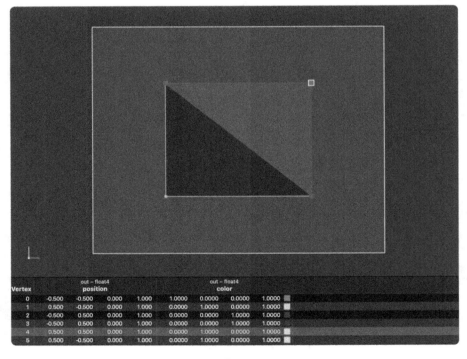

Figure 6-11. *Metal View debugger showing vertices of a rectangle*

Figure 6-12. *Rendered rectangle*

Figure 6-11 is a screenshot of the Metal View debugger. It features six points; each one is a vertex of a triangle.

Another interesting detail: colors are interpolated into the gradient, even in the composite shape drawn from multiple figures.

Perspective Projection Transformation

So, let's implement the matrix described in the "Understanding the Math" section.

1. Open the `Matrix + Transformations.swift` file
   and add another initialization method to the matrix
   4x4 structure.

```
init(perspective fovY: Float, aspect: Float, near:
Float = 0.01, far: Float = 100) {
    let fovY = (fovY * 0.5).cgFloat.degreesTo
    Radians().float
    let yScale = 1 / tan(fovY)
    let xScale = yScale / aspect
    let zRange = far - near
    let zScale = far / zRange
    let wzScale = -near * far / zRange

    let X = SIMD4<Float>(xScale, 0, 0, 0)
    let Y = SIMD4<Float>(0, yScale, 0, 0)
    let Z = SIMD4<Float>(0, 0, zScale, 1)
    let W = SIMD4<Float>(0, 0, wzScale, 0)

    matrix_float_4x4.init(columns: (X, Y, Z, W))
}
```

This code is identical to the calculations described
in the "Understanding the Math" section.

2. Insert the `projectionTransformationMatrix` class
   variable and update the `setupBindings()` function
   in the `ProjectionTransformationRenderingTool.
   swift` file.

```
private var projectionTransformationMatrix:
matrix_float4x4

init() {
    ...
```

```
    self.projectionTransformationMatrix =
    matrix_float4x4(perspective: 180, aspect: 1.0)
}

private func setupBindings() {
    $fov.removeDuplicates().combineLatest($aspect.
    removeDuplicates())
        .map({ matrix_float4x4(perspective: $0.0,
        aspect: $0.1) })
        .assign(to: \.projectionTransformationMatrix,
        on: self)
        .store(in: &matricesBindings)
    ...
}
```

This variable is a container for the transformation
matrix generated by the current perspective and
aspect ratio level.

3. Update the shader function to receive the matrix
    and update the **vertex** position according to the
    selected projection.

```
vertex VertexOut matrixTransformVertexShader(const
device VertexIn *vertices [[buffer(0)]],
                            constant float4x4
                            &transformMatrix [[buffer(1)]],
                            constant float4x4
                            &projectionMatrix
                            [[buffer(2)]],
                            uint vid [[vertex_id]]) {
    VertexOut outVertex;
    VertexIn inVertex = vertices[vid];
```

```
outVertex.position = projectionMatrix *
transformMatrix * inVertex.position;
outVertex.color = inVertex.color;

return outVertex;
}
```

Note that the order of the applicable transformations is highly important, and you can't change the position of the matrix factors.

4. When `projectionTransformationMatrix` is calculated, and the shader function can receive it as an argument, convert the matrix to the buffer by inserting the following code in the `handleRenderEncoder` function of the `ProjectionTransformationRenderingTool` class.

```
encoder.setVertexBytes(&projectionTransformationMatrix,
                length: MemoryLayout
                <matrix_float4x4>.stride,
                index: 2)
```

5. Build and run your project.

When the translation along the Z axis is zero, the rendering result does not display properly in perspective. Figure 6-13 illustrates an empty rendering result due to the absence of Z translation.

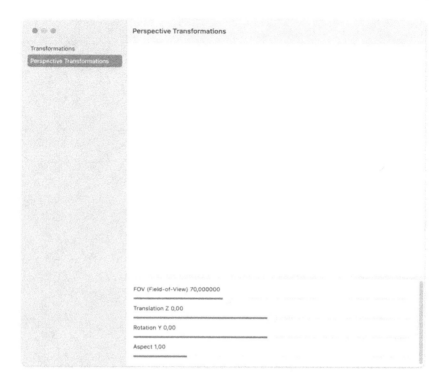

Figure 6-13. *Empty rendering result due to zero Z translation*

Try to increase the `translationZ` argument. Figure 6-14 shows this perspective scaling effect.

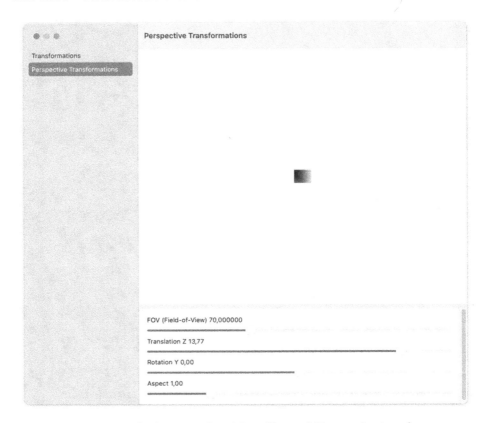

Figure 6-14. *Rendering result with adjusted Z translation for perspective scaling*

To avoid future inconvenience, let's just set the default `translationZ` value.

```
init() {
    ...
    self.translationZ = 3.0
    ...
}
```

Now, you have just made a scale. Does it make sense if you can achieve the same result with a much simpler transformation based on translationX and translationY parameters?

It does if you can rotate the camera point of view around.

Rotate the Perspective Projection Around the Eye Position

Figure 6-15 represents eye position relative to the viewing frustum.

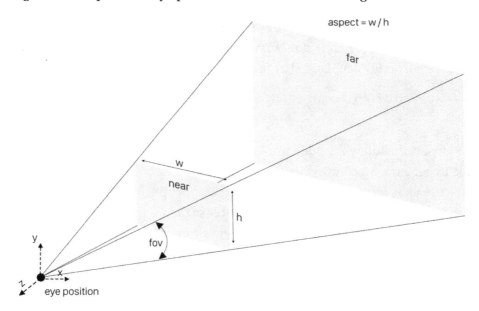

Figure 6-15. *Diagram showing eye position relative to the viewing frustum*

The eye position transformation requires another matrix to calculate the final vertex position.

```
init(cameraEyePosition eyePosition: simd_float3,
targetPosition: simd_float3 = .init(.zero, .zero, .zero),
upVector: simd_float3 = .init(0.0, 1.0, 0.0)) {
    let forwardVector = normalize(targetPosition - eyePosition)
    let rightVector = normalize(cross(upVector, forwardVector))
    let upVector = cross(forwardVector, rightVector)

    let X = SIMD4<Float>(rightVector.x, rightVector.y,
    rightVector.z, -dot(rightVector, eyePosition))
    let Y = SIMD4<Float>(upVector.x, upVector.y,
    upVector.z, -dot(upVector, eyePosition))
    let Z = SIMD4<Float>(forwardVector.x, forwardVector.y,
    forwardVector.z, -dot(forwardVector, eyePosition))
    let W = SIMD4<Float>(0, 0, 0, 1)

    self.init(columns: (X, Y, Z, W))
}
```

Insert the following code into the `Matrix + Transformations.swift` file to get a transformation matrix required for changing the eye position.

The view matrix is derived from the camera's position (**eyePosition**), the target position it's looking at (**targetPosition**), and a specified up vector (upVector) that defines the camera's vertical direction.

Given the vectors calculated in the function.

- **forwardVector** is the normalized direction vector from the eye position to the target position.

- **rightVector** is the normalized vector perpendicular to both the upVector and forwardVector.

- **upVector** (redefined) is the cross-product of forwardVector and rightVector, ensuring it's orthogonal to both.

These vectors define the orientation of the camera in world space. The translation component (the position of the camera in the world) is encoded in the matrix by the dot products of the orientation vectors with the negative eye position (**-dot(...)** terms). This effectively translates world coordinates to the camera's local coordinate system.

The resulting matrix is shown in Figure 6-16.

$$\begin{bmatrix} r_x & u_x & f_x & 0 \\ r_y & u_y & f_y & 0 \\ r_z & u_z & f_z & 0 \\ -d(r \cdot e) & -d(u \cdot e) & -d(f \cdot e) & 1 \end{bmatrix}$$

Figure 6-16. *Matrix for transforming the camera's eye position*

- r_x, r_y, r_z are the components of rightVector.

- u_x, u_y, u_z are the components of upVector (redefined).

- f_x, f_y, f_z are the components of forwardVector.

- e is the eyePosition.

Next, to make the view transformations work, update the shader function in the TransformShader.metal file.

```
vertex VertexOut matrixProjectionTransformVertexShader(const
device VertexIn *vertices [[buffer(0)]],
           constant float4x4 &transformMatrix [[buffer(1)]],
           constant float4x4 &projectionMatrix [[buffer(2)]],
           constant float4x4 &viewMatrix [[buffer(3)]],
           uint vid [[vertex_id]]) {
```

```
    VertexOut outVertex;
    VertexIn inVertex = vertices[vid];

    outVertex.position = projectionMatrix * viewMatrix *
    transformMatrix * inVertex.position;
    outVertex.color = inVertex.color;

    return outVertex;
}
```

Insert the EyePosition struct and the eyePosition class variable to the ProjectionTransformationRenderingTool class.

```
struct EyePosition: Equatable {
    var x: Float
    var y: Float
    var z: Float

    var simd: SIMD3<Float> {
        return SIMD3(x, y, z)
    }

    static func == (lhs: EyePosition, rhs: EyePosition) -> Bool {
        return lhs.simd == rhs.simd
    }
}

@Published var eyePosition: EyePosition

init() {
...
self.eyePosition = .init(x: .zero, y: .zero, z: -5.0)
...
}
```

Update the stack of sliders in the `ProjectionTransformationView.swift` file to make changes in the `eyePosition` coordinates.

```
...
VStack(alignment: .leading, spacing: 4.0) {
    Text("FOV (Field-of-View) \(renderingTool.fov,
    specifier: "%f")")
    Slider(value: $renderingTool.fov, in: 15.0 ... 180.0)
    Text("Translation Z \(renderingTool.translationZ,
    specifier: "%.2f")")
    Slider(value: $renderingTool.translationZ, in: -20.0
    ... 20.0)
    Text("Rotation Y \(renderingTool.rotationY, specifier:
    "%.2f")")
    Slider(value: $renderingTool.rotationY, in: -20.0 ... 20.0)
    Text("Eye Position X \(renderingTool.eyePosition.x,
    specifier: "%.2f")")
    Slider(value: $renderingTool.eyePosition.x, in:
    -20.0 ... 20.0)
    Text("Eye Position Y \(renderingTool.eyePosition.y,
    specifier: "%.2f")")
    Slider(value: $renderingTool.eyePosition.y, in:
    -20.0 ... 20.0)
    Text("Eye Position Z \(renderingTool.eyePosition.z,
    specifier: "%.2f")")
    Slider(value: $renderingTool.eyePosition.z, in:
    -10.0 ... 0.0)
    Text("Aspect \(renderingTool.aspect, specifier: "%.2f")")
    Slider(value: $renderingTool.aspect, in: 0.0 ... 5.0)
}
...
```

With the following code you make a sliders subscribed to the
@Published eye position variable.

The final step is to use the eyePosition variable as a
vertex shader function argument. Let's make it by inserting the
following code into the handleRenderEncoder function of the
ProjectionTransformationRenderingTool class.

```
var viewMatrix = matrix_float4x4(cameraEyePosition: self.
eyePosition.simd)
encoder.setVertexBytes(&viewMatrix,
                       length: MemoryLayout<matrix_float4x4>.
                       stride,
                       index: 3)
```

Run your project. Play with different eye positions (see Figures 6-17
and 6-18).

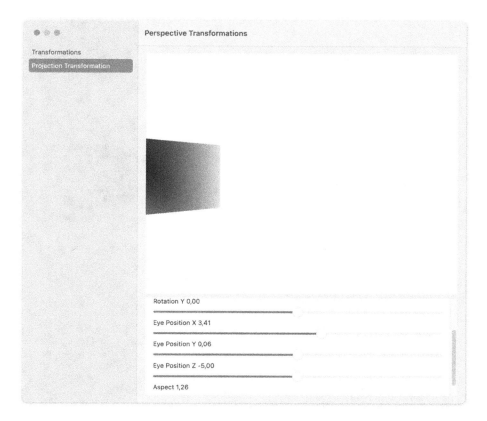

Figure 6-17. *Eye Position X update, similar to human's eye looking to the left*

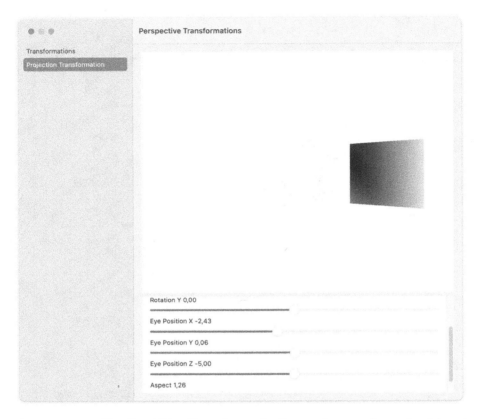

Figure 6-18. *Eye Position X update, similar to human's eye looking to the right*

Conclusion

This chapter explored perspective transformations and how they can be implemented. The following are the key points.

- The field of view, aspect ratio, and the near and far variables are used to calculate the projection transformation matrix.

- Implementing perspective transformations involves creating and adjusting various matrices, including the transformation matrix and the projection matrix.

- The concept of an "eye position" allows you to change the camera's viewpoint, which can make objects appear to be viewed from different angles and distances.

CHAPTER 7

Working with Textures and Images

You have already used buffers to pass data to the GPU and draw primitives. But, if you need to store and manipulate images on the GPU, you need something more structured than a buffer, offering advanced possibilities in terms of memory management.

Creating Texture

To create a new texture, first, create an `MTLTextureDescriptor` object. This class is a container for properties that specify the texture's layout, format, and access permissions.

```
let textureDescriptor = MTLTextureDescriptor()
```

Pixel Format

```
textureDescriptor.pixelFormat = .bgra8Unorm
```

In this example, `pixelFormat` is set to `.bgra8Unorm`, which means that bits are arranged into 8 bits per component in **blue**, **green**, **red**, and **alpha** order, as illustrated in Figure 7-1.

© Bogdan Redkin and Victor Yaskevich 2024
B. Redkin and V. Yaskevich, *Master Photo and Video Editing with Metal*,
https://doi.org/10.1007/979-8-8688-0832-6_7

Figure 7-1. *Bits in .bgra8Unorm pixel format*

There are three pixel formats: ordinary, packed, and compressed. For ordinary and packed formats, the name of the pixel format specifies the order of components (such as R, RG, RGB, RGBA, BGRA), bits per component (such as 8, 16, 32), and data type for the component (such as Float, Sint, Snorm, Uint, Unorm).

If the pixel format name has the _sRGB suffix, reading and writing pixel data applies sRGB gamma compression and decompression. The alpha component of sRGB pixel formats is always treated as a linear value. The differences in color mapping are explored later; for now, let's use .bgra8Unorm for rendering texture.

Storage Mode

Storage mode defines how a resource's memory is managed and accessed by the CPI and GPU. Storage mode for texture can be set by the following code:

```
textureDescriptor.storageMode = MTLStorageMode.private
```

- MTLStorageMode.managed: On macOS, it allows CPU read and write access with required synchronization. Figure 7-2 represents this storage mode.

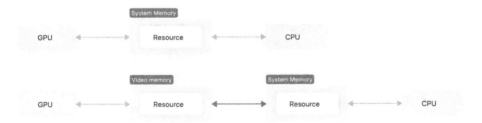

Figure 7-2. *MTLStorageMode.managed*

- MTLStorageMode.private: It is for GPU-only accessible textures requiring staging resources for updates. Figure 7-3 represents this storage mode.

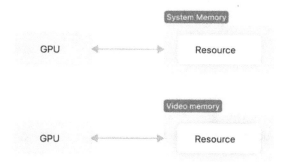

Figure 7-3. *MTLStorageMode.private*

- MTLStorageMode.shared: It is available on iOS and Apple silicon Macs for shared CPU and GPU access; synchronization management is still necessary to avoid race conditions. Figure 7-4 represents this storage mode.

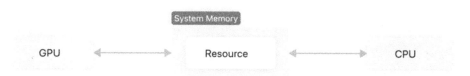

Figure 7-4. *MTLStorageMode.shared*

Usage

The usage of textures also affects their performance. Textures configured with the .renderTarget flag are optimized for writing but perform worse in reading operations.

Create Texture

You can create the texture once you have defined the pixel format, usage, and storage mode. But before that, you have to set the texture size and type. This book focuses only on 2D textures because it concentrates on image editing.

```
textureDescriptor.textureType = .type2D
textureDescriptor.width = 256
textureDescriptor.height = 256
let texture = device.makeTexture(descriptor: textureDescriptor)!
```

With the `makeTexture` function, Metal creates `MTLTexture` and allocates memory for it, but it doesn't contain any data.

In the example project, you read the image data and fill the texture with it. Then, you map the texture onto the transformable rectangle from the previous chapter.

Note   Another option for creating MTLTexture from the image is to iterate on every pixel inside the source image and copy byte per byte to the destination image data, so loading textureData directly from disk is the easiest way.

The Starter Project

The starter project includes the same transformations as the previous chapter but with a few updates.

- UI interface now has an image picker to update rendering texture with selected images.

- TextureVertex is a new model with texture coordinates support.

Load Texture from UIImage

The MetalKit framework provides a great class to make creating MTLTexture from an image URL much easier: MTKTextureLoader.

Let's start with the updates in the TextureProjectionTransformation RenderingTool class by adding an update(texture:) function and an MTLTexture class variable.

```
private(set) var texture: MTLTexture?

func update(texture: MTLTexture?) {
    self.texture = texture
    guard let texture else { return }
    self.aspect = (canvasSize.width / canvasSize.height).float
    * (texture.height.float / texture.width.float)
}
```

The aspect variable will be updated based on the new aspect ratio.

Then you need to implement a creation of texture from the selected image. To do so, open TextureProjectionTransformationView.swift and update the ImagePicker selection handler.

```
ImagePicker(title: "Choose Image", handler: { url in
    do {
        let texture = try MTKTextureLoader(device: device).
        newTexture(URL: url)
        texture.label = "selected_image"
        self.renderingTool.update(texture: texture)
    } catch {
        print("texture loading error: \(error)")
    }
})
```

The following code uses MTKTextureLoader to fetch texture data from the selected URL. Then texture is labeled as "selected_image" for easier access in the Metal debugger. After that, TextureProjectionTransformationRenderingTool is updated with the selected texture.

Display Texture

Unlike UIImageView, you can't just render a texture in metal canvas. MTLTexture doesn't have position or frame; it contains only image data, which describes pixels and colors inside them.

Remember how you made a rectangle in Chapter 6 that rendered colored vertices from two triangles into a smooth gradient? The rendering of a texture works similarly, but you must map vertex coordinates with texture coordinates.

As discussed in Chapter 5, texture coordinates represented a value from 0.0 to 1.0 in both the x and y directions, so you must map the pixel position with the texture position.

To simplify these operations, your starter project includes a TextureVertex model. Let's take a look at it.

```
struct TextureVertex {
    enum Corner {
        case topLeft, topRight, bottomLeft, bottomRight
    }

    var position: vector_float2
    var texcoord: vector_float2

    init(position: vector_float2, texcoord: vector_float2) {
        self.position = position
        self.texcoord = texcoord
    }
```

```
init(corner: Corner) {
    switch corner {
    case .topLeft:
        self.init(position: .init(x: -1.0, y: 1.0),
        texcoord: .init(0.0, 0.0))
    case .topRight:
        self.init(position: .init(x: 1.0, y: 1.0),
        texcoord: .init(1.0, 0.0))
    case .bottomLeft:
        self.init(position: .init(x: -1, y: -1), texcoord:
        .init(0.0, 1.0))
    case .bottomRight:
        self.init(position: .init(x: 1, y: -1), texcoord:
        .init(1.0, 1.0))
    }
  }
}
```

It has a designed initializer with the Corner enum, and each corner
have its own representation in pixel coordinate, and texture coordinate,
which makes initializing process straightforward.

```
TextureVertex(corner: .bottomRight)
```

Let's use the new TextureVertex structure to draw a simple rectangle.
First, create a pair of triangles in the handleRenderEncoder method of the
TextureProjectionTransformationRenderingTool class.

```
func handleRenderEncoder(encoder: MTLRenderCommandEncoder,
metalView mtkView: MTKView, viewportSize: CGSize) {

    ...
    //setViewport
    ...
```

```
let textureVertices: [TextureVertex] = [
    .init(corner: .bottomRight),
    .init(corner: .bottomLeft),
    .init(corner: .topLeft),
    .init(corner: .bottomRight),
    .init(corner: .topRight),
    .init(corner: .topLeft)
]

let buffer = device.makeBuffer(
    bytes: textureVertices,
    length: MemoryLayout<TextureVertex>.stride *
    textureVertices.count,
    options: .storageModeShared
)

encoder.setVertexBuffer(buffer, offset: 0, index: 0)
    ...
    //drawPrimitives
}
```

Build and run your project. Select any image by pressing the **Choose Image** button. The rendering result initially appears as a black rectangle with the aspect ratio of the selected image, as shown in Figure 7-5.

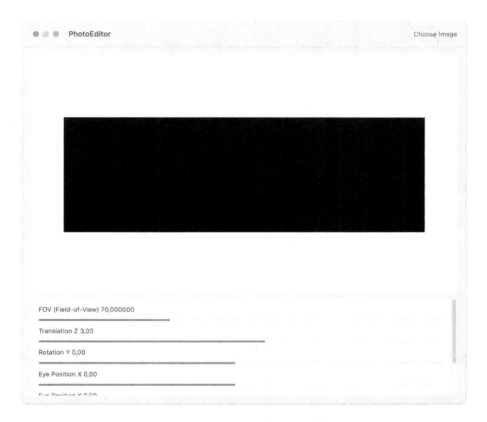

Figure 7-5. *The initial rendering result shows a black rectangle with the aspect ratio of the selected image*

In the result, you should see a black rectangle with the aspect ratio of the selected image. *But why?*

The following describes what happens when you select an image.

1. You make a texture with MTKTextureLoader and send it to TextureProjectionTransformation RenderingTool.

2. In the update(texture: MTLTexture?) function, you update the aspect variable, which is used in a projectionTransformationMatrix calculation.

3. projectionTransformationMatrix is sent to texture
   ProjectionTransformVertexShader and transforms
   the vertex position; thus, the shape of the rendering
   result is updated.

4. The textureVertices array creates a rectangle
   from two triangles and then fills with color from the
   textureFragmentShader function.

5. Since the textureFragmentShader function returns
   float4(0,0,0,1);, the color of each pixel was black.

And that explains the resulting black rectangle with the aspect ratio of
the selected image.

So, what must you do to fill this rectangle with a texture? Update
textureFragmentShader to replace the black color with the color from the
texture.

Sampling

The process of calculating the color of a texture at the texture coordinates
is called **sampling** because it takes a sample of texture data.

So, the fragment function needs to be extended with two arguments.

- TexturePipelineRasterizerData in [[stage_in]] is
  a set of parameters from the rasterizer stage,
  including the texture coordinates—texcoord.

- texture2d<float> texture [[texture(0)]] is a
  texture to sample.

Update a fragment function in the TextureShader.metal file.

```
 fragment float4 textureFragmentShader(Texture
PipelineRasterizerData in [[stage_in]],
texture2d<float> texture [[texture(0)]])
{
    constexpr sampler textureSampler(mag_filter::linear,
min_filter::linear);
    float4 colorSample = float4(texture.sample(
textureSampler, in.texcoord));
    return colorSample;
}
```

This code creates textureSampler, which describes how you want to sample the texture. The sample() function fetches one or more pixels from the texture and returns a color calculated from those pixels.

- mag_filter: a type of magnification. Magnification happens when the rendering area is larger than the size of the texture. It has two options.

- **linear** selects two pixels in each dimension and interpolates linearly between them.

- **nearest** selects the single pixel nearest to the sample point.

- min_filter: a type of minification. Minification happens when the rendering area is smaller than the size of the texture. It has the same options as mag_filter.

After the required arguments are declared in the fragment function, there is only one step left: pass the texture as an argument to the fragment function.

Insert this line in the `handleRenderEncoder` function of the `TextureProjectionTransformationRenderingTool` class.

```
encoder.setFragmentTexture(texture, index: 0)
```

Build and run your project, and select any image. Figure 7-6 shows the result of applying the texture, which supports the same transformations as a rectangle from the previous chapter.

Figure 7-6. *Final rendered texture with applied transformations*

The result is that you rendered a texture, and it supports the same transformations as a rectangle from Chapter 6.

Conclusion

This chapter explored how to create, apply, and store textures.

Textures can serve as input and output resources to shader functions, allowing you to reuse textures between multiple pipelines.

Textures are filled with pixels, and each pixel contains colors. The property that describes the number of color bits and their order is `pixelFormat`.

PART II

Image Editing with Metal

CHAPTER 8

Basic Color Adjustments

Introduction to Compute Shaders

In the previous chapter, you loaded an image and displayed it on the screen using the rasterization pipeline, composed of vertex and fragment shaders applied to triangles.

Now, let's explore a new type of shader pipeline: compute shaders. The compute pipeline is much simpler than the rasterization pipeline. Essentially, you declare a function and specify how many times to call it. Each invocation receives its own index, enabling you to select different data to process. Moreover, these invocations are massively parallel in the GPU, enhancing the efficiency of executing such workloads.

Given that an image consists of individual pixels that can be processed independently, compute shaders are an ideal choice for applying effects. Compute shaders are used to do the following.

- Adjust the image's contrast, brightness, and saturation

- Apply effects such as vignette, blur, and distortion

- Modify colors using color lookup tables (LUT)

© Bogdan Redkin and Victor Yaskevich 2024
B. Redkin and V. Yaskevich, *Master Photo and Video Editing with Metal*,
https://doi.org/10.1007/979-8-8688-0832-6_8

Image Effect Abstraction

To have a universal effect interface, you need to define its protocol.

```
/// Universal interface for the image effect.
protocol EffectPass {
    /// Record commands into command buffer for the effect.
    ///
    /// @param target Texture to read input from and write
        output to.
    func writeCommands(cb: MTLCommandBuffer, target:
    MTLTexture)
}
```

The protocol is quite straightforward and requires the implementation of only a single function. Let's examine it in detail. When you declare a new class for the image effect, it must record commands into the command buffer to create the effect. You supply the cb parameter for the implementation to record commands. You also provide the target texture, which contains the image data to be modified by the compute shader.

Contrast, Brightness, Saturation Effects

Let's use an example to demonstrate how to adjust an image's contrast, brightness, and saturation.

Initial Setup

Before writing shader logic to modify image pixels directly, you need to set up the Swift side. Let's create a class for the effect.

```
/// Effect pass to adjust contrast, saturation, brightness.
final class ContrastBrightnessSaturationEffect: EffectPass {
```

CHAPTER 8   BASIC COLOR ADJUSTMENTS

```
private let device: MTLDevice
private let computePipeline: MTLComputePipelineState

init(device: MTLDevice) throws {
    self.device = device

    let shadersLibrary = device.makeDefaultLibrary()!

    // The name of our compute shader function in .metal file,
    // we will proceed to define it in just a minute.
    let shaderName = "contrastBrightnessSaturationCS"

    let shader = shadersLibrary.makeFunction(name:
                shaderName)!

    self.computePipeline
        = try device.makeComputePipelineState(function:
          shader)
}

func writeCommands(cb: MTLCommandBuffer, target:
MTLTexture) {
    // We will fill that with code later.
}
}
```

To create a compute pipeline, call device.makeComputePipelineStat
e(function: shader) with the shader you want the pipeline to use. Now,
let's declare the shader itself.

```
// Shader to adjust contrast, brightness, saturation.
kernel void contrastBrightnessSaturationCS(
    texture2d<float, access::read_write> targetTexture
    [[texture(0)]],
    uint2 gid [[thread_position_in_grid]]
```

```
) {
    // NOTE: currently, the shader doesn't have anything
    // to do with contrast, brightness, saturation.
    // Let's have some time to set up some things first

    float3 rgb = targetTexture.read(gid).rgb;

    // Change the RGB color in any way you want.
    // As an example, we will invert the color.
    float3 updatedRgb = 1.0 - rgb;

    targetTexture.write(float4(updatedRgb, 1.0), gid);
}
```

Let's look at the function parameters. The first parameter is the texture that you will modify, which involves reading and writing data to it.

Notice how we handle data in the image. Previous chapters utilized samplers to retrieve color from the image. As more complex objects, samplers offer additional features that aren't necessary in this context. This example uses the read function to load the pixel value directly at the x, y offset. Similarly, the write function stores the provided value in the texture. Remember, to make these operations possible, the texture must be created with .usage containing both .shaderRead and .shaderWrite flags.

Compute Pipeline Grid, Threads, and Thread Groups

As briefly mentioned, the compute shader operates over a grid. This grid is three-dimensional, but for 2D image processing, the depth of the grid is generally set to 1.

In Metal terminology, each invocation of your shader function is called a **thread**. For instance, if you have a 1920x1080 image, you must execute the shader function for each pixel, requiring a grid of size MTLSize(width: 1920, height: 1080, depth: 1).

For the sake of hardware optimizations, threads are organized into **threadgroups**. A threadgroup comprises several threads that execute together and can optionally share a common block of memory. When working with images, a threadgroup represents a chunk of the image grid (see Figure 8-1). When you dispatch a compute command, you provide a count of threadgroups and a count of threads within each group. The resulting grid size is threadgroupsCount * threadsPerThreadgroup.

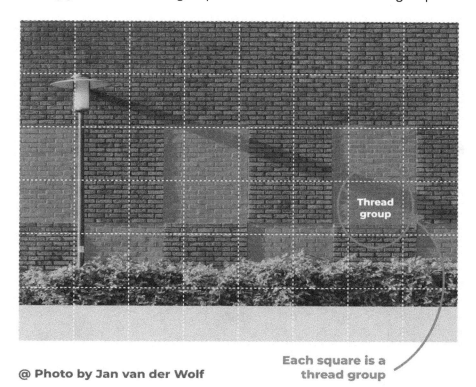

@ **Photo by Jan van der Wolf**

Each square is a thread group

Figure 8-1. *Compute thread grid visualization*

Note   The resulting grid from the command dispatch call may exceed the actual image size. You can check whether the current thread index in the grid falls within the image bounds. However, it's generally fine to ignore out-of-bound access in shaders.

Examine the gid parameter in the shader, which is annotated with the [[thread_position_in_grid]] attribute. It represents the index of the current shader invocation, or thread, within the grid. If the dispatch yields a grid size of MTLSize(width: 1920, height: 1080, depth: 1), gid.x is in the 0..<1920, range and gid.y is in the 0..<1080 range. These indices access individual pixels from the texture.

Dispatch Computing Commands

Let's complete the writeCommands method in the ContrastBrightnessSaturationEffect class.

```
func writeCommands(cb: MTLCommandBuffer, target: MTLTexture) {
    // Make the compute encoder.
    guard let computeEncoder
        = cb.makeComputeCommandEncoder() else { return }

    // Bind our compute pipeline state to the encoder.
    computeEncoder.setComputePipelineState(self.computePipeline)

    // Bind the texture that we are going to modify.
    computeEncoder.setTexture(target, index: 0)

    // Here is the actual part of dispatching the compute
    command:

    // How many threads in the thread group we are dispatching.
    let workgroup = MTLSize(
```

```
        width: computePipeline.threadExecutionWidth,
        height: computePipeline.maxTotalThreadsPerThreadgroup
                / computePipeline.threadExecutionWidth,
        depth: 1
    )

    // Make the grid size from the image we process.
    let imageSize = MTLSize(
        width: target.width,
        height: target.height,
        depth: target.depth
    )

    // This call encodes a compute dispatch command.
    //
    // First parameter is a count of thread groups we create,
    // the second is the count of threads
    // in the individual threadgroup.
    computeEncoder.dispatchThreadgroups(
        // Dispatch enough groups to cover the entire grid.
        divUp(imageSize, workgroup),
        threadsPerThreadgroup: workgroup
    )

    // Finish compute encoding.
    computeEncoder.endEncoding()
}
// ...


/// Ceiling division, e.g. `divUp(10, 3)` is `4`.
func divUp(_ lhs: Int, _ rhs: Int) -> Int {
    (lhs + rhs - 1) / rhs
}
```

```
/// Same, but for all components of `MTLSize`.
func divUp(_ lhs: MTLSize, _ rhs: MTLSize) -> MTLSize {
    MTLSize(
        width: divUp(lhs.width, rhs.width),
        height: divUp(lhs.height, rhs.height),
        depth: divUp(lhs.depth, rhs.depth)
    )
}
```

Although we could have chosen any random value for the threadgroup size, like 16x16, 32x32, or 64x64, we followed the recommendation from Metal. Metal advises that the threadgroup size should be a multiple of the pipeline's `threadExecutionWidth`. The `maxTotalThreadsPerThreadgroup` represents the maximum number of threads in a threadgroup.

Now, if you call the `writeCommands` method with the image displayed on the screen as a target, the image is inverted, as shown in Figure 8-2.

Figure 8-2. *Image inverted by the compute shader*

The image colors were successfully inverted.

Implementing Contrast, Brightness, Saturation Shader

Now, let's proceed with the actual implementation of color adjustments.

Linear vs. Gamma Color Space

Before manipulating colors, you need to consider the color space you use. The EffectPass abstraction establishes that the texture colors you read and write are in the **linear** color space. For textures in sRGB formats, the shader reads and writes are automatically converted by the hardware to function in linear space while storing gamma space data in memory. So, if you correctly select the texture format according to its content, you won't need to perform additional conversions.

Adjusting Contrast and Brightness

The following function is used to adjust the contrast and brightness of individual pixels.

```
float3 applyContrastBrightness(
    float3 rgb,
    float contrast,
    float brightness
) {
    float3 newColor = contrast * (rgb - 0.5) + 0.5 + brightness;
    return clamp(newColor, 0.0, 1.0);
}
```

Contrast adjustment operates by computing the deviation from the mean value (`rgb - 0.5`). This deviation is then scaled with the `contrast` factor and added to the mean value.

Brightness is added to the color, increasing the value toward white.

These adjustments can cause overflow beyond 1.0, so clamping the result to an acceptable range is necessary.

Adjusting Saturation

We won't directly manipulate the RGB values to adjust saturation as we did with contrast and brightness. Instead, let's convert the image to the **HSL** (hue, saturation, and lightness) color model. The saturation component of this model is indeed what we need to adjust.

```
float3 hsl = colors::rgbToHsl(rgb);

// Scale the saturation component by our saturation factor.
hsl[1] *= saturation;

float3 finalColor = colors::hslToRgb(hsl);
```

The `rgbToHsl` and `hslToRgb` functions can be found in the appendix.

Combine the Shader Components

The following is the final version of the `contrastBrightnessSaturationCS` shader.

```
 #include <metal_stdlib>
using namespace metal;

#include "../../CommonShaders/Colors.h"

#include "./ContrastBrightnessSaturationSettings.h"
```

```
float3 applyContrastBrightness(
    float3 rgb,
    float contrast,
    float brightness
) {
    float3 newColor = contrast * (rgb - 0.5) + 0.5 +
    brightness;
    return clamp(newColor, 0.0, 1.0);
}

// Shader to adjust contrast, brightness, saturation.
<ernel void contrastBrightnessSaturationCS(
    texture2d<float, access::read_write> targetTexture
    [[texture(0)]],
    uint2 gid [[thread_position_in_grid]],
    constant ContrastBrightnessSaturationSettings* settings
                            [[buffer(0)]]
) {
    float3 rgb = targetTexture.read(gid).rgb;

    // Apply contrast and brightness.
    rgb = applyContrastBrightness(
        rgb, settings->contrast,
        settings->brightness
    );

    // Convert to HSL.
    float3 hsl = colors::rgbToHsl(rgb);

    // Adjust saturation.
    hsl[1] *= settings->saturation;
```

```
// Convert back to RGB.
float3 finalColor = colors::hslToRgb(hsl);

targetTexture.write(float4(finalColor, 1.0), gid);
}
```

You may have noticed that we added a third parameter to the shader. This is because we want to provide adjustment factors from the Swift side and need to pass these settings to the shader.

We defined a common structure for providing settings to the shader. It was achieved by creating a `ContrastBrightnessSaturationSettings.h` file with the following content.

```
#ifndef ContrastBrightnessSaturationSettings_h
#define ContrastBrightnessSaturationSettings_h

struct ContrastBrightnessSaturationSettings {
    float contrast;
    float brightness;
    float saturation;
};

#endif /* ContrastBrightnessSaturationSettings_h */
```

The shader expects the `ContrastBrightnessSaturationSettings` value in the buffer at index 0. You must bind the byte data of this struct value to the shader. To accomplish this, add the following line to the `writeCommands` implementation immediately after the line where you bind the target texture. Remember to include this `.h` file in your bridging header, enabling Swift to generate a wrapper for it.

```
var settings = ContrastBrightnessSaturationSettings(
    contrast: 2.0,
    brightness: -0.2,
    saturation: 0.5
)
```

```
computeEncoder.setBytes(
    &settings,
    length: MemoryLayout<ContrastBrightnessSaturationSettings>.
    size,
    index: 0
)
```

Now, you can execute the program and observe the results (see Figure 8-3).

Figure 8-3. *High contrast, desaturated image computed by the shader*

Try playing with different contrast, brightness, and saturation values.

Conclusion

This chapter mainly served as an introduction to the GPU compute pipeline. You learned about the computational model, how to write shaders, and how to interact with it from Swift.

The upcoming chapters continue implementing different effects using the EffectPass protocol. This universal interface allows you to compose multiple effects and build a multilayer photo editor.

CHAPTER 9

Vignettes

A **vignette** is a popular technique in which the edges and corners of an image are made darker than the center. This technique is widely used in photography and image editing to control viewer focus and enhance the overall composition of the image.

Creating a Vignette Effect

The objective is to darken the corners of an image. How can this be accomplished? Since RGB components represent brightness values in each channel, you simply need to scale them uniformly to reduce them.

First, let's reduce the brightness of the pixels by a constant value, for instance, 0.5 in this example.

Darkening Pixels

Let's create the kernel shader to modify the image pixels. Put this into the VignetteShader.metal file.

```
#include <metal_stdlib>
using namespace metal;

kernel void applyVignette(
    // The texture we modify.
```

© Bogdan Redkin and Victor Yaskevich 2024
B. Redkin and V. Yaskevich, *Master Photo and Video Editing with Metal*,
https://doi.org/10.1007/979-8-8688-0832-6_9

```
  texture2d<float, access::read_write> targetTexture
  [[texture(0)]],
  // Pixel coordinates.
  uint2 gid [[thread_position_in_grid]]
) {
    // Read pixel we want to modify.
    float3 rgb = targetTexture.read(gid).rgb;

    // Let it be constant for now.
    float darkeningFactor = 0.5;

    // Apply darkening factor.
    float3 finalColor = rgb * darkeningFactor;

    // Write the result to the texture.
    targetTexture.write(float4(finalColor, 1.0), gid);
}
```

And here's the `EffectPass` implementation.

```
final class VignetteEffect: EffectPass {
    private let device: MTLDevice
    private let computePipeline: MTLComputePipelineState

    init(device: MTLDevice) throws {
        self.device = device

        let shadersLibrary = device.makeDefaultLibrary()!

        // Create compute pipeline with our `applyVignette`
        // kernel shader.

        self.computePipeline = try device.makeCompute
        PipelineState(
            function: shadersLibrary.makeFunction(
                name: "applyVignette"
```

```
        )!
    )
}

var name: String {
    "Vignette"
}

func writeCommands(cb: MTLCommandBuffer, target:
MTLTexture) {
    guard let computeEncoder
        = cb.makeComputeCommandEncoder() else { return }

    // Bind the pipeline to use our shader.
    computeEncoder.setComputePipelineState(self.compute
    Pipeline)

    // Bind our target texture.
    computeEncoder.setTexture(target, index: 0)

    let workgroup = MTLSize(
        width: computePipeline.threadExecutionWidth,
        height: computePipeline.maxTotalThreadsPer
                Threadgroup /
                computePipeline.threadExecutionWidth,
        depth: 1
    )
    let imageSize = MTLSize(
        width: target.width,
        height: target.height,
        depth: target.depth
    )
```

```
computeEncoder.dispatchThreadgroups(
    divUp(imageSize, workgroup),
    threadsPerThreadgroup: workgroup
)

computeEncoder.endEncoding()
    }
}
```

Let's run it. The result is shown in Figure 9-1.

Figure 9-1. *Image, darkened by 50% in shader*

A constant of 0.5 is used as the darkening factor, which makes the entire image appear darker. To darken only the pixels in the corners, you need to calculate the factor dynamically for each pixel based on its position.

Calculating the Radial Factor

First, let's calculate the texture coordinates of the pixel.

```
// UV coordinates of the current pixel.
float2 uv = float2(gid) / float2(
    targetTexture.get_width(),
    targetTexture.get_height()
);
```

Let's output it for visual inspection.

```
// UV coordinates of the current pixel.
float2 uv = float2(gid) / float2(targetTexture.get_width(),
targetTexture.get_height());

targetTexture.write(float4(uv, 1.0, 1.0), gid);

// ...

// Don't forget to comment the code which is currently writes the
// output:
// targetTexture.write(float4(finalColor, 1.0), gid);
```

You should expect something like what's shown in Figure 9-2. The top left corner should be blue; the top right should be magenta; the bottom right should be white; and the bottom left should be cyan.

Figure 9-2. *Colored visualization of the texture UV coordinates*

Now that you have the pixel coordinates, you can calculate the distance from the pixel to the center using the metal::distance function. Its purpose is to calculate the distance between two points.

```
// Calculate the distance from the center of the texture.
// Our UV coordinates are in range from 0.0 to 1.0,
// so the center is at 0.5.
float distance = metal::distance(uv, float2(0.5, 0.5));
```

Figure 9-3 is a visualization of the calculated distance.

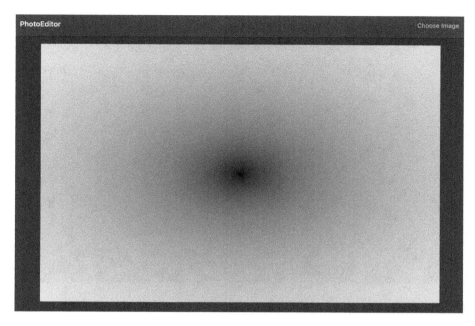

Figure 9-3. *Visualization of the distance from the pixel to the center*

Final Result

Now, you can use it as a darkening factor for the image pixels.

```
// NOTE: we need to inverse the distance.
// The greater the distance, the lower the darkening
// factor should be.
float darkeningFactor = 1.0 - distance;

// Apply darkening factor.
float3 finalColor = rgb * darkeningFactor;
```

Let's run it. Figure 9-4 displays the results.

159

Figure 9-4. *Result of darkening image using distance to the center as a factor*

The current results are too weak. The effect needs to be adjusted. During the pixel distance calculation from the center, you can experiment with your own algorithms to determine the darkening factor. Any method that suits your artistic preference will work. This book examines the smoothstep function to control the vignette effect.

The smoothstep function is very useful in computer graphics. It smoothly interpolates values within a specific interval and clamps them when they go beyond this range.

For example, smoothstep(0.4, 1.3, x) would appear like this: values ranging from 0.4 to 1.3 are smoothly interpolated, while other values are clamped (see Figure 9-5).

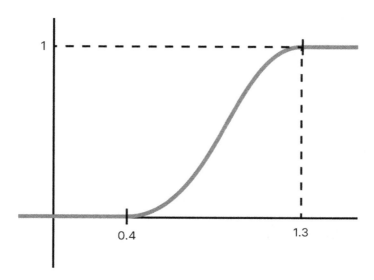

Figure 9-5. *Smoothstep function visualization*

Let's add two parameters to the vignette shader. Declare a structure for the settings in the VignetteSettings.h file.

```
struct VignetteSettings {
    // Distance at which the vignette effect starts;
    // in UV units from the center.
    float offset;
    // Distance of spread of the vignette effect; in UV units.
    float softness;
};
```

Include this function in the bridging header to use it from Swift.

In the writeCommands function, you must bind the data to the shader.

```
var settings = VignetteSettings(offset: 0.3, softness: 0.6)

// Bind settings data.

computeEncoder.setBytes(
```

```
    &settings,
    length: MemoryLayout<VignetteSettings>.size,
    index: 0
)
```

Then, use these parameters in the shader.

```
#include <metal_stdlib>
using namespace metal;

// NOTE: Don't forget to include the definition
// of our settings structure.
#include "./VignetteSettings.h"

kernel void applyVignette(
    // The texture we modify.
    texture2d<float, access::read_write> targetTexture
    [[texture(0)]],
    // Pixel coordinates.
    uint2 gid [[thread_position_in_grid]],
    // Effect settings.
    constant VignetteSettings* settings [[buffer(0)]]
) {
    if (
        gid.x < targetTexture.get_width()
        && gid.y < targetTexture.get_height()
    ) {
        // Read pixel we want to modify.
        float3 rgb = targetTexture.read(gid).rgb;

        // Calculate the distance from the center of the
        texture.
        // Our UV coordinates are in range from 0.0 to 1.0,
        //so the center is at 0.5.
```

```
float distance = metal::distance(uv, float2(0.5, 0.5));

// Adjust the distance with smoothstep function.
distance = smoothstep(
    settings->offset,
    settings->offset + settings->softness,
    distance
);

// Let it be constant for now.
float darkeningFactor = 1.0 - distance;

// Apply darkening factor.
float3 finalColor = rgb * darkeningFactor;

// Write the result to the texture.
targetTexture.write(float4(finalColor, 1.0), gid);
    }
}
```

The result has much more contrast, as seen in Figure 9-6.

Figure 9-6. *More intense darkening achieved with smoothstep function*

You can adjust the settings to achieve varying levels of vignette intensity.

Conclusion

Creating a vignette effect is a great example of how pixel shaders can manipulate images directly. By darkening the corners of the image, the vignette effect allows you to guide the viewer's focus toward the center, enhancing the overall image composition.

Using Metal to implement the effect enables you to easily adjust the vignette shader's parameters. This kind of fine-grained control is one of the many advantages of using shaders in image processing. However, the vignette effect is just one of many image-processing effects that can be achieved through shaders. With a good understanding of shader programming and a bit of creativity, you can create a wide range of effects to enhance and manipulate your images.

The next chapter explores more advanced shader programming techniques and how they can be used to create even more complex and interesting image effects.

CHAPTER 10

Blur

A blur is the effect of combining each pixel's color with the colors of its neighboring pixels. This technique smooths out sharp edges and details, producing a softer, uniform appearance. It's akin to blending colors on a canvas, where each color spot influences its surroundings to create a gentle, blurred effect.

How Is the Blur Effect Achieved?

In brief, this is accomplished by blending surrounding pixels.

In terms of image processing, blur is a **convolution filter**.

A convolution filter adjusts each pixel in the image based on the colors of surrounding pixels and a weighted grid for these pixels.

This "weighted grid" is referred to as a **convolution kernel**.

Picture this kernel moving across the image. At each point, it examines the central pixel and its neighbors, multiplies the color value by the corresponding weight from the kernel, and adds up the results. These kernels are useful not only for blurring but also for sharpening details or detecting edges.

It's important to note that the weights in the blur kernels must total 1.0 to prevent changes in the brightness of the output image.

© Bogdan Redkin and Victor Yaskevich 2024
B. Redkin and V. Yaskevich, *Master Photo and Video Editing with Metal*,
https://doi.org/10.1007/979-8-8688-0832-6_10

Box Blur

The simplest form of blur is achieved by averaging the pixels. This means making all weights in the kernel equal. This method is called a **box blur** (see Figure 10-1).

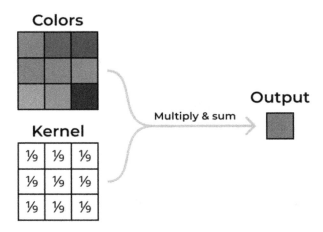

Figure 10-1. *Box blur algorithm*

The following sample code demonstrates a box blur.

```
// NOTE: this is a pseudocode.
```

```
// Total count of pixels in kernel.
let pixelsInKernel = kernelSize * kernelSize
```

```
// We combine all pixels within the kernel together,
// where each pixel contributes equally.
let weight = 1.0 / pixelsInKernel
```

```
// Set output to zero.
var output = Color(0.0, 0.0, 0.0)
```

```
for x in 0..<kernelSize {
    for y in 0..<kernelSize {
```

```
    output += image[x, y] * weight
  }
}
```

Figure 10-2 shows this applied to an image.

Figure 10-2. *Image, blurred using box blur algorithm*

As you can see, the blurred image isn't very smooth. This is because each pixel in the kernel contributes equally to the output. For a smoother blur, distant pixels should contribute less to the output. Therefore, the **convolution kernel** should assign lower weights to pixels closer to the edge.

Gaussian Function

Let's assign smaller weights to lower the influence of distant values on the output (see Figure 10-3).

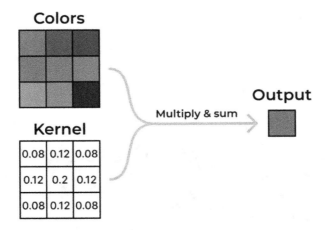

Figure 10-3. *Gaussian blur algorithm*

To achieve this, you utilize the **Gaussian function**. If you graph it (see Figure 10-4), you can observe that the values farther from the center are smaller. This function is also known as a **bell-shaped** function.

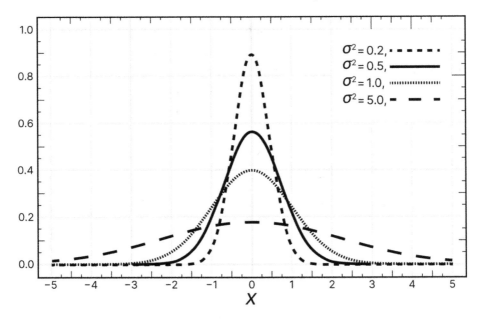

Figure 10-4. *Gaussian function graph*

Adjusting the Blur Intensity

The Gaussian function is parameterized by **σ (sigma)**.

Sigma is a parameter in the Gaussian function, often called the **standard deviation**. It controls the steepness of the resulting distribution.

In the context of adjusting blur, the sigma parameter determines the intensity of the blur. By altering sigma, you control the point at which the function's output values become so small that they barely affect the result.

Calculating Weights

The following formula calculates the weights for the kernel.

$$G(x,y) = \frac{1}{2\pi\sigma^2} e^{-\frac{x^2+y^2}{2\sigma^2}}$$

The following code also calculates the weights for the kernel.

```
func gaussianWeight(x: Float, y: Float, sigma: Float)
-> Float {
    let exponent = -(x * x + y * y) / (2 * sigma * sigma)
    let coefficient = 1 / (2 * Float.pi * sigma * sigma)
    return coefficient * exp(exponent)
}
```

Kernel Size for Gaussian Blur

Although **sigma** is related to the blur radius, it doesn't dictate the kernel size directly.

Ideally, because the Gaussian function extends infinitely, an infinite kernel size is required to sample all its values.

However, in practical application, the influence of distant Gaussian values progressively decreases. Therefore, only a segment of the Gaussian curve needs to be covered, disregarding values that are too distant and contribute insignificantly.

```
// NOTE: this is a pseudocode.

let sigma = 20.0

// To calculate kernel radius, we will just scale it by the
multiplier.
// That is simple and works well. Good values are from
2.0 to 3.0.
let multiplier = 2.5

let kernelRadius = Int(ceil(sigma * multiplier))

let kernelSize = kernelRadius + 1 + kernelRadius

// Since we sampling only segment of the curve,
// the kernel values will not sum up to 1.0.
// So we need to fix it manually.
var sumWeights = 0.0
for x in -kernelRadius...kernelRadius {
    for y in 0..<kernelSize {
        sumWeights += gaussianWeight(Float(x), Float(y), sigma)
    }
}

// Set output to zero.
var output = Color(0.0, 0.0, 0.0)

for x in -kernelRadius...kernelRadius {
    for y in -kernelRadius...kernelRadius {
        let w = gaussianWeight(
            Float(x),
```

```
        Float(y),
        sigma
    ) / sumWeights
    output += image[x, y] * w
  }
}
```

When applied to an image, the Gaussian blur appears much smoother to the eye than the box blur, as seen in Figure 10-5.

Box blur   **Gaussian blur**

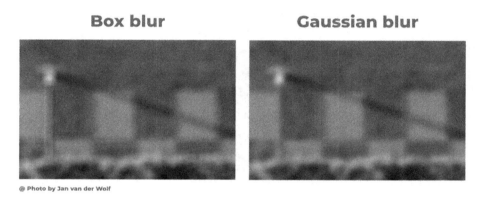

@ Photo by Jan van der Wolf

Figure 10-5. *Box blur vs. Gaussian blur comparison*

Advanced GPU Implementation

Now, let's implement the Gaussian blur algorithm on a GPU.

Although a GPU is a powerful device, the naive Gaussian blur algorithm has exponential complexity. This means that if you set the blurring radius too large, even the GPU may be unable to handle it.

Separable Filters

The fundamental concept of a blurring algorithm involves blending all values within a 2D kernel. This can quickly become a significant issue, particularly when applying intense blur. If the kernel size is n, the number of texture samples required is n^2. And that's just for one pixel! For instance, for a 4K image with a kernel size of 21, the number of texture samples would be 21 * 21 * 4096 * 2160 = 3,901,685,760. This is too much for the GPU to manage.

Fortunately, you can restructure computations to reduce the complexity from $O(n^2)$ to $O(n)$. The Gaussian function is popular for blurring algorithms not only because it appears smooth but also because it is **separable**.

A separable filter is an operation that can be represented as a product of several other operations. In image processing, some 2D kernels can be represented as two 1D kernels applied sequentially. This reduces the complexity from $O(n^2)$ to $O(n)$.

In this case, $G(x, y)$ can be represented as $G(x) * G(y)$, where

$$G(x) = \frac{1}{\sqrt{2\pi\sigma^2}} e^{-\frac{x^2}{2\sigma^2}}$$

To confirm, try multiplying them manually.

The blur is divided into two passes: vertically and horizontally. The order of the passes is not important; they just need to be separate so that the second pass operates on the output of the first. Additionally, only a single 1D kernel is needed because the same $G(x)$ function is used for both passes.

Figure 10-6 presents the result of the first blur pass.

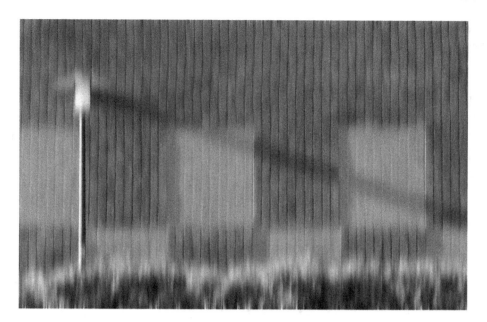

Figure 10-6. *Vertical pass of optimized Gaussian blur algorithm*

Shader

Sampler Configuration

You need to sample pixels in all directions within a certain kernel. For edge pixels, some samples may exceed texture bounds. To address this, set `address::clamp_to_edge`. This action clamps your sample coordinates to texture bounds, returning the color of the image edge.

Additionally, `coord::pixel` is used to utilize pixel coordinates as UV values.

```
constexpr sampler textureSampler(
    address::clamp_to_edge,
    coord::pixel
);
```

Providing Data to the Shader

If you look at the formula $G(x) = \dfrac{1}{\sqrt{2\pi\sigma^2}} e^{-\frac{x^2}{2\sigma^2}}$, you see that the input x is only used as x^2, which erases the sign from the input, making $G(x) = G(-x)$. Thus, the kernel is mirrored around its center, which means only one side of its data needs to be sent to the GPU. This portion is known as the **kernel half-size**. Let's use the trailing side of the kernel—the side where the x values approach the positive direction.

Let's send two parameters to the GPU shader: kernel half-size and kernel data.

Kernel data is a pointer to sequential float values in memory. The count of these values equals the kernel half-size.

```
float3 calculateGaussianBlur(
    // Texture coordinates of the pixels we calculate the
    blur for.
    // This coordinates are in pixels.
    float2 uv,
    int kernelHalfSize,
    constant float *weights,
    // Texture we sample the colors of surrounding pixels from.
    texture2d<float, access::sample> blurSrc,
    // Direction of the blur. For horizontal blur it's
    float2(1, 0),
    // for vertical blur it's float2(0, 1).
    float2 direction
) {
    // Define the sampler we use to sample the texture.
    constexpr sampler textureSampler(
        filter::linear,
        address::clamp_to_edge,
```

```
        coord::pixel
    );

    // Start with the center pixel.
    float3 value
        = blurSrc.sample(textureSampler, uv).rgb * weights[0];

    // Then apply the surrounding pixels.
    for (int i = 1; i < kernelHalfSize; i++) {
        // Since we provide GPU with only half of the kernel,
        // we apply the samples from both sides.
        // The side we apply the samples from is determined
        // by the direction of the blur.
        // For vertical blur we apply samples from the top
        // and bottom side of the center pixel.
        // For horizontal blur we apply samples from the left
        // and right side of the center pixel.

        // UV of the pixel on the bottom/right side
        // of the center pixel.
        float2 uv1 = uv + float(i) * direction;
        value += blurSrc.sample(textureSampler, uv1).rgb
                 * weights[i];

        // UV of the pixel on the top/left side of the
        center pixel.
        float2 uv2 = uv - float(i) * direction;
        value +=
            blurSrc.sample(textureSampler, uv2).rgb *
            weights[i];
    }

    return value;
}
```

The following is the code for the vertical and horizontal compute shaders.

```
kernel void gaussianBlurVerticalCS(
    texture2d<float, access::write> output [[texture(0)]],
    texture2d<float, access::sample> blurSrc [[texture(1)]],
    uint2 gid [[thread_position_in_grid]],
    constant int *kernelHalfSize [[buffer(0)]],
    constant float *weights [[buffer(1)]]
) {

    // UV coordinates of the current pixel
    // (not normalized, in pixels).
    // It is calculated by adding 0.5 to the integer
    pixel offset,
    // so the UV coordinates are in the center of the pixel.
    float2 uv = float2(gid) + float2(0.5, 0.5);;

    float3 value = calculateGaussianBlur(
        uv, *kernelHalfSize, weights, offsets,
        blurSrc, float2(0.0, 1.0)
    );

    output.write(float4(value, 1.0), gid);
}

kernel void gaussianBlurHorizontalCS(
    texture2d<float, access::write> output [[texture(0)]],
    texture2d<float, access::sample> blurSrc [[texture(1)]],
    uint2 gid [[thread_position_in_grid]],
    constant int *kernelHalfSize [[buffer(0)]],
    constant float *weights [[buffer(1)]]
) {
    // UV coordinates of the current pixel
```

```
// (not normalized, in pixels).
// It is calculated by adding 0.5 to the integer
pixel offset,
// so the UV coordinates are in the center of the pixel.
float2 uv = float2(gid) + float2(0.5, 0.5);;

float3 value = calculateGaussianBlur(
    uv, *kernelHalfSize, weights, offsets,
    blurSrc, float2(1.0, 0.0)
);

output.write(float4(value, 1.0), gid);
}
```

You've completed the GPU shaders. Now, let's move on to the CPU part.

First, you need to calculate the Gaussian kernel.

```
// Calculate the 1D gaussian kernel.
//
// The resulting arrays contains center and weight from
// the trailing size of the kernel, because
// the full gaussian kernel is mirrored.
func gaussianKernel(sigma: Float, multiplier: Float) ->
[Float] {
    // Gaussian function does not expect 0 as sigma value.
    // Handle this case manually.
    if sigma == 0.0 {
        return [1.0]
    }

    let halfSize = 1 + Int(ceil(sigma * multiplier))

    var kernel: [Float] = []
```

```
    for i in 0..<halfSize {
        let x = Float(i)

        let exponent = -(x * x) / (2 * sigma * sigma)
        let coefficient = 1 / (sqrt(2 * Float.pi) * sigma)
        let w = coefficient * exp(exponent)

        kernel.append(w)
    }

    // Sum the kernel values

    var sum = kernel[0] // Value in center of the kernel

    for k in kernel[1...] {
        // We don't store both sides of the kernel,
        // since it is mirrored.
        // So we need to add value from both sides, i.e.
        double it.
        sum += k * 2.0
    }

    // Normalize the kernel.
    // We need all kernel values to sum up to 1.0

    let normalizedKernel = kernel.map { $0 / sum }

    return normalizedKernel
}
```

Let's encapsulate the "state" of the Gaussian kernel into a separate structure for convenience.

```
struct GaussianBlurKernel {
    // NOTE: Full gaussian kernel is mirrored, we store only
    center + trailing edge.
```

```
let weights: [Float]

init(sigma: Float, multiplier: Float = 2.5) {
    self.weights
        = gaussianKernel(sigma: sigma, multiplier:
          multiplier)
}

var halfSize: Int {
    self.weights.count
}

// The amount of samples we need to do for each pixel.
var samplesCount: Int {
    self.halfSize * 2 - 1
}
}
```

Now implement EffectPass in Swift.

```
final class GaussianBlurEffect: EffectPass {
    private let device: MTLDevice

    private let computePipelineV: MTLComputePipelineState
    private let computePipelineH: MTLComputePipelineState

    private var blurIntermediate: MTLTexture? = nil

    var kernel: GaussianBlurKernel = GaussianBlurKernel(
        radius: 10.0, sizeMultiplier: 2.0
    )

    init(device: MTLDevice) throws {
        self.device = device

        let shadersLibrary = device.makeDefaultLibrary()!
```

```
    self.computePipelineV = try device.makeCompute
    PipelineState(
        function: shadersLibrary.makeFunction(
            name: "gaussianBlurVerticalCS"
        )!
    )
    self.computePipelineH = try device.makeComputePipeline
                            State(
        function: shadersLibrary.makeFunction(
            name: "gaussianBlurHorizontalCS"
        )!
    )
}

var name: String {
    "Gaussian blur"
}

func writePass(
    cb: MTLCommandBuffer,
    pipeline: MTLComputePipelineState,
    blurSrc: MTLTexture, blurOutput: MTLTexture
) {
    guard let encoder
        = cb.makeComputeCommandEncoder() else { return }

    encoder.setComputePipelineState(pipeline)

    encoder.setTexture(blurOutput, index: 0)

    encoder.setTexture(blurSrc, index: 1)

    var kernelSize: Int32 = Int32(self.kernel.kernelSize)
    var weights: [Float] = self.kernel.weights
```

```
var offsets: [Float] = self.kernel.offsets

encoder.setBytes(
    &kernelSize, length: MemoryLayout<Int32>.size,
    index: 0
)

encoder.setBytes(
    &weights,
    length:
        MemoryLayout<Float>.stride * self.kernel.
        kernelSize,
    index: 1
)

let workgroup = MTLSize(
    width: pipeline.threadExecutionWidth,
    height: pipeline.maxTotalThreadsPerThreadgroup
            / pipeline.threadExecutionWidth,
    depth: 1
)

let imageSize = MTLSize(
    width: blurOutput.width,
    height: blurOutput.height,
    depth: blurOutput.depth
)

encoder.dispatchThreadgroups(
    divUp(imageSize, workgroup),
    threadsPerThreadgroup: workgroup
)

encoder.endEncoding()
}
```

```
func writeCommands(cb: MTLCommandBuffer, target:
MTLTexture) {
    let blurIntermediate: MTLTexture

    // Try reuse intermediate texture
    if let bi = self.blurIntermediate,
       bi.width == target.width,
       bi.height == target.height,
       bi.pixelFormat == target.pixelFormat
    {
        blurIntermediate = bi
    } else {
        let blurIntermediateDesc =
            MTLTextureDescriptor.texture2DDescriptor(
                pixelFormat: target.pixelFormat,
                width: target.width,
                height: target.height,
                mipmapped: false
            )
        blurIntermediateDesc.usage = [.shaderWrite,
                                      .shaderRead]
        blurIntermediate = device.makeTexture(
            descriptor: blurIntermediateDesc
        )!
        self.blurIntermediate = blurIntermediate
    }

    self.writePass(
        cb: cb, pipeline: self.computePipelineV,
        blurSrc: target, blurOutput: blurIntermediate
    )

    self.writePass(
```

```
        cb: cb, pipeline: self.computePipelineH,
        blurSrc: blurIntermediate, blurOutput: target
    )
  }
}
```

You've successfully implemented two-pass Gaussian blurring on the GPU.

The complexity of the algorithm has been reduced from quadratic to linear. Let's recalculate the optimization metric, which is the number of texture samples in the shader for a 4K image with 21 pixels. Now it's 2 * 21 * 4096 * 2160 = 371589120, which is ten times fewer than we previously had.

But performance can be improved even further!

Sample Two Pixels at Once

Texture samplers don't just read the direct value of a pixel. They can also sample between pixels. This process is known as **linear sampling**. The value is linearly interpolated from the nearest pixels to the sampling point. This functionality is built into the GPU hardware, so it's virtually cost-free.

A GPU shader sums values multiplied by weight, which is what linear sampling does.

For instance, let's say that

- p1 is the color at coordinates float2(100, 100)

- p2 is the color at coordinates float2(101, 100)

If you sample the value at coordinates float2(100.3, 100), the output of the sampled value will be as follows.

```
t = 0.3
p = p1 * (1.0 - t) + p2 * t =  p1 * 0.7 + p2 * 0.3
```

To take advantage of this opportunity, let's calculate the offset value from the sampled kernel center.

$$w12 = w1 + w2$$

$$\textit{offset}(o1,o2) = \frac{w1 * o1 + w2 * o2}{w12}$$

Here is this formula written in Swift.

```swift
func mergeWeights(
    w1: Float,
    w2: Float,
    o1: Float,
    o2: Float
) -> (Float, Float) {
    let w12 = w1 + w2
    let o = (w1 * o1 + w2 * o2) / w12
    return (w12, o)
}
```

Here, $w1$ and $o1$ represent the weight and offsets of the first weight to be merged, while $w2$ and $o2$ represent the weight and offsets of the second weight.

Let's write a function that merges adjacent weights using the earlier method.

```swift
func optimizeKernel(
    weights oldWeights: [Float]
) -> ([Float], [Float]) {
    var weights: [Float] = [oldWeights[0]]
    var offsets: [Float] = [0.0]

    var i = 1
```

```
while i < oldWeights.count {
    let hasNext = (i + 1) < oldWeights.count

    if hasNext {
        let w1 = oldWeights[i]
        let w2 = oldWeights[i + 1]

        let (w, o) = mergeWeights(
            w1: w1,
            w2: w2,
            o1: Float(i),
            o2: Float(i + 1)
        )

        weights.append(w)
        offsets.append(o)

        i += 2
    } else {
        weights.append(oldWeights[i])
        offsets.append(Float(i))

        i += 1
    }
}

return (weights, offsets)
}
```

Now, let's update GaussianBlurKernel to use this optimization.

```
struct GaussianBlurKernel {
    // NOTE: Full gaussian kernel is mirrored,
    // we store only center + trailing edge.
    let weights: [Float]
```

```
    let offsets: [Float]

    init(sigma: Float, multiplier: Float = 2.5) {
        let kernel = gaussianKernel(
            sigma: sigma, multiplier: multiplier
        )

        let (w, o) = optimizeKernel(weights: kernel)

        assert(w.count == o.count)

        self.weights = w
        self.offsets = o
    }

    var halfSize: Int {
        self.weights.count
    }

    // The amount of samples we need to do for each pixel.
    var samplesCount: Int {
        self.halfSize * 2 - 1
    }
}
```

Modify the shader to use the new offsets.

```
float3 calculateGaussianBlur(
    // Texture coordinates of the pixels we calculate
    // the blur for. These coordinates are in pixels.
    float2 uv,
    int kernelHalfSize,
    constant float *weights,
    constant float *offsets,
```

```
    // Texture we sample the colors of
    // surrounding pixels from.
    texture2d<float, access::sample> blurSrc,
    // Direction of the blur.
    // For horizontal blur it's float2(1, 0),
    // for vertical blur it's float2(0, 1).
    float2 direction
) {
    // Define the sampler we use to sample the texture.
    constexpr sampler textureSampler(
        filter::linear,
        address::clamp_to_edge,
        coord::pixel
    );

    // Start with the center pixel.
    float3 value = blurSrc.sample(
        textureSampler, uv
    ).rgb * weights[0];

    // Then apply the surrounding pixels.
    for (int i = 1; i < kernelHalfSize; i++) {
        // Since we provide GPU with only half of the kernel,
        // we apply the samples from both sides.
        // The side we apply the samples from is determined by
        // the direction of the blur.
        // For vertical blur we apply samples from the top and
        // bottom side of the center pixel.
        // For horizontal blur we apply samples from the left
        // and right side of the center pixel.

        // UV of the pixel on the bottom/right
        // side of the center pixel.
```

```
        float2 uv1 = uv + offsets[i] * direction;
        value += blurSrc.sample(
            textureSampler, uv1
        ).rgb * weights[i];

        // UV of the pixel on the top/left side
        // of the center pixel.
        float2 uv2 = uv - offsets[i] * direction;
        value += blurSrc.sample(
            textureSampler, uv2
        ).rgb * weights[i];
    }

    return value;
}
```

Don't forget to bind the new offset data to the shader.

```
// ...

encoder.setBytes(
    &kernelSize, length: MemoryLayout<Int32>.size, index: 0
)
encoder.setBytes(
  &weights,
  length: MemoryLayout<Float>.stride * self.kernel.kernelSize,
  index: 1
)
encoder.setBytes(
  &offsets,
  length: MemoryLayout<Float>.stride * self.kernel.kernelSize,
  index: 2
)

// ...
```

You've completed the optimization. The straightforward but effective strategy of combining adjacent samples significantly reduces the number of samples needed. This optimization has allowed you to cut the required samples by almost half. This practical and efficient method enables you to process larger images in real time.

Conclusion

The chapter began by discussing the concept and method of Gaussian blur, then implemented it on the GPU. The naive method led to exponential complexity, which could make even powerful devices struggle when processing larger images.

This issue was overcome by leveraging the separable nature of the Gaussian function, which allowed you to reduce the complexity from $O(n^2)$ to $O(n)$. This was a significant improvement, but we didn't stop there. We further optimized the process by using the GPU's hardware capability for linear sampling, combining adjacent samples to reduce the number of samples needed by almost half.

In this chapter, you learned how to work with the Gaussian function, implement and optimize a Gaussian blur algorithm on a GPU, and make your graphics more efficient and effective. If you plan on implementing a Gaussian blur in your project, follow this guide to avoid common pitfalls and make your implementation as efficient as possible.

CHAPTER 11

Lookup Table

A color **lookup table** (LUT) maps one color value to another. These tables are typically encoded as a texture, with the pixels containing the destination color. The coordinates for sampling this color are derived from the source color value.

LUT images can vary in layout. The most common format is depicted in Figure 11-1. Note that this is a no-op LUT, meaning it maps the color to itself.

Figure 11-1. *LUT texture that maps the color to itself*

© Bogdan Redkin and Victor Yaskevich 2024
B. Redkin and V. Yaskevich, *Master Photo and Video Editing with Metal*,
https://doi.org/10.1007/979-8-8688-0832-6_11

Calculating Color Coordinates in LUT Texture

The LUT is a 512x512 pixel image containing an 8x8 grid of quads. The blue channel selects a quad. The red and green channels act as X and Y coordinates within that quad to determine the final color. With 8x8, or 64 quads, each quad being 64x64 pixels, there are 64 values for each channel to encode color mapping information. Colors between these points are blended according to the source color position.

Sampling a LUT Texture

Let's create a function to sample a LUT texture.

```
// Find a new color that corresponds to the input color
// in the 2D grid `lutTexture`.
// NOTE: The input color must be in sRGB format.
// Returns linear color.
float3 lookup(
    float3 color,
    texture2d<float, access::sample> lutTexture
) {
    // Define sampler we will use for LUT sampling.
    constexpr sampler lutSampler(
        mag_filter::linear, min_filter::linear
    );

    float gridSide = 8.0; // Our grid is 8x8 quads.
    float gridQuads = gridSide * gridSide; // Our grid
    is square.

    // Find which quad to use, using blue color.
```

```
float quadIndex = color.b * (gridQuads - 1.0);

// Note: since LUT quad resolution is only 64,
// we need to blend between its points.
// That's why we select two quads.

float2 quad1;
// Y quad offset.
quad1.y = floor(floor(quadIndex) / gridSide);
// X quad offset.
quad1.x = floor(quadIndex) - (quad1.y * gridSide);

float2 quad2;
// Y quad offset.
quad2.y = floor(ceil(quadIndex) / gridSide);
// X quad offset.
quad2.x = ceil(quadIndex) - (quad2.y * gridSide);

// Calculate UV coordinates for sampling.

float2 texScale = float2(
    1.0 / lutTexture.get_width(),
    1.0 / lutTexture.get_height()
);
// We do sample in normalized UV coordinates, so we use
// this value to adjust sampling point to the pixel center.
float2 pixelCenter = 0.5 * texScale;

// Offset in UV space within the quad.
float2 inQuadUvOffset = color.rg / gridSide + pixelCenter;

float2 uv1 = quad1 / gridSide + inQuadUvOffset;
float2 uv2 = quad2 / gridSide + inQuadUvOffset;

// Sample colors and mix samples from quads.
```

```
    float3 newColor1 = lutTexture.sample(lutSampler, uv1).rgb;
    float3 newColor2 = lutTexture.sample(lutSampler, uv2).rgb;

    float3 newColor = mix(
        newColor1,
        newColor2,
        float(fract(quadIndex))
    );

    return newColor;
}
```

Creating a Shader and Effect Pass

Now, let's incorporate it into the shader kernel. Note that the source color is converted to sRGB. This is necessary because the corresponding color coordinates are positioned in sRGB.

The linearToSRGB function can be found in the appendix.

```
#include "../../CommonShaders/Colors.h"

kernel void lutColorCorrection(
    texture2d<float, access::read_write> targetTexture
[[texture(0)]],
    texture2d<float> lutTexture [[texture(1)]],
    uint2 gid [[thread_position_in_grid]],
    constant float* intensity [[buffer(0)]]
) {
    float3 rgb = targetTexture.read(gid).rgb;

    // Since colors in LUT table are positioned in gamma space,
    // we need to convert it to gamma space
    float3 srgb = colors::linearToSRGB(rgb);
```

```
    float3 newRgb = lookup(srgb, lutTexture);

    // NOTE: we mixing `rgb` and `newRgb`.
    // Both are linear rgb, not sRGB,
    // because `lookup` returns linear color.
    float3 finalColor = mix(rgb, newRgb, *intensity);

    targetTexture.write(float4(finalColor, 1.0), gid);
}
```

Now, let's switch to the Swift side and create
LutColorCorrectionEffect.

```
final class LutColorCorrectionEffect: EffectPass {
    private let device: MTLDevice
    private let computePipeline: MTLComputePipelineState
    private var lut: MTLTexture?

    var intensity: Float

    init(device: MTLDevice, intensity: Float = 1.0) throws {
        self.device = device

        let shadersLibrary = device.makeDefaultLibrary()!

        self.computePipeline = try device.makeCompute
        PipelineState(
            function: shadersLibrary.makeFunction(
                name: "lutColorCorrection"
            )!
        )

        self.lut = nil

        self.intensity = intensity
```

```
    }

    func loadLut(_ url: URL) throws {
        self.lut = try MTKTextureLoader(
            device: self.device
        ).newTexture(URL: url)
    }

    var name: String {
        "LUT Color Correction"
    }

    func writeCommands(cb: MTLCommandBuffer, target:
MTLTexture) {
        // If no LUT is loaded, don't apply any effect
        guard let lut = self.lut else { return }

        guard let computeEncoder
            = cb.makeComputeCommandEncoder() else { return }

        computeEncoder.setComputePipelineState(self.compute
        Pipeline)

        computeEncoder.setTexture(target, index: 0)
        computeEncoder.setTexture(lut, index: 1)

        var intensity = simd_float1(self.intensity);
        computeEncoder.setBytes(
            &intensity,
            length: MemoryLayout<simd_float1>.size,
            index: 0
        )

        let workgroup = MTLSize(
            width: computePipeline.threadExecutionWidth,
```

```
        height: computePipeline.maxTotalThreadsPer
        Threadgroup
                / computePipeline.threadExecutionWidth,
        depth: 1
    )

    let imageSize = MTLSize(
        width: target.width,
        height: target.height,
        depth: target.depth
    )

    computeEncoder.dispatchThreadgroups(
        divUp(imageSize, workgroup),
        threadsPerThreadgroup: workgroup
    )

    computeEncoder.endEncoding()
    }
}
```

Final Results

You might have noticed a no-op LUT texture at the beginning of the article. However, a real LUT that transforms the color would look like Figure 11-2.

Figure 11-2. *LUT texture that makes colors more pale and blue-ish*

Let's load this and apply it to the test image.

Figure 11-3 shows the original image with no LUT applied.

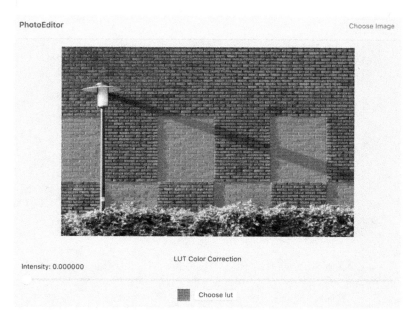

Figure 11-3. *Original image with no applied LUT*

Figure 11-4 shows the image with LUT applied.

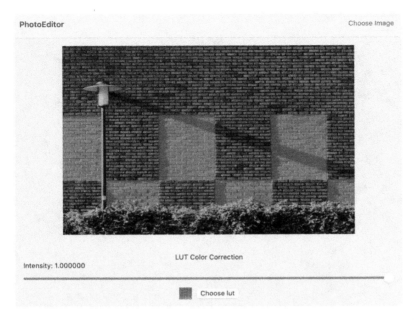

Figure 11-4. *Image with LUT applied by the compute shader*

Conclusion

LUTs are powerful tools for color correction and grading. They allow you to map input color values to new output values, effectively transforming the color space of an image. This is especially useful in image editing, game development, film production, and any other visual field where precise control over color is paramount.

This chapter explored the fundamentals of LUTs, how to calculate color coordinates in a LUT texture, how to sample a LUT texture, and finally, how to integrate it into the shader kernel. You also saw the dramatic changes a LUT can make to an image, transforming its color space to create a different visual effect.

CHAPTER 12

Twirl

Displacement Effects

Displacement effects refer to the effects that cause pixels in an image to shift to a different position based on certain rules. Examples of such effects include warp, pinch, bump, and twirl.

The **twirl** displacement effect (see Figure 12-1) gives the appearance of pixels rotating around a specific point in the image. This chapter focuses on implementing this effect using the Metal compute shader and the `EffectPass` abstraction.

© Bogdan Redkin and Victor Yaskevich 2024
B. Redkin and V. Yaskevich, *Master Photo and Video Editing with Metal*,
https://doi.org/10.1007/979-8-8688-0832-6_12

Figure 12-1. *An example of the twirl displacement effect*

Create a Twirl Effect

Twirl Settings

To start, let's create a settings structure for the twirl effect. There are two parameters: radius and angle. Create a TwirlSettings.h file and include it in your bridging header.

```
#ifndef TwirlSettings_h
#define TwirlSettings_h

struct TwirlSettings {
    // Radius of the twirl, in UV units.
```

```
    float radius;
    // Angle of the twirl.
    float angle;
};

#endif /* TwirlSettings_h */
```

Twirl Effect Pass

The important aspect here is pixel displacement. This means the pixel you read might differ from the one you write. This modification doesn't occur within a single compute shader thread, so you need to separate the texture you write to and the texture you sample for pixel data. The first one serves as the output target, modified by the shader. The second one remains unmodified, allowing you to safely sample any pixel from it.

The second texture is cached to prevent having to create it every frame.

```
final class TwirlEffect: EffectPass {
    private let device: MTLDevice

    private let computePipeline: MTLComputePipelineState

    // The cached second texture we were talking about.
    private var intermediateTexture: MTLTexture? = nil

    var settings: TwirlSettings

    init(device: MTLDevice) throws {
        self.device = device

        let shadersLibrary = device.makeDefaultLibrary()!

        self.computePipeline = try device.makeCompute
        PipelineState(
            function: shadersLibrary.makeFunction(
```

```
            name: "twirlCS"
        )!
    )

    self.settings = TwirlSettings(
        radius: 0.25, angle: 3.14 / 4.0
    );
}

var name: String {
    "Twirl"
}

func writeCommands(cb: MTLCommandBuffer, target:
                    MTLTexture) {
    let intermediateTexture: MTLTexture

    // Try reuse intermediate texture
    if let i = self.intermediateTexture,
       i.width == target.width,
       i.height == target.height,
       i.pixelFormat == target.pixelFormat
    {
        intermediateTexture = i
    } else {
        let intermediateTextureDesc =
            MTLTextureDescriptor.texture2DDescriptor(
                pixelFormat: target.pixelFormat,
                width: target.width,
                height: target.height,
                mipmapped: false
            )
        intermediateTexture = device.makeTexture(
            descriptor: intermediateTextureDesc
```

```
    )!
    self.intermediateTexture = intermediateTexture
}

guard let blitEncoder = cb.makeBlitCommandEncoder()
                        else {
    return
}

blitEncoder.copy(from: target, to: intermediateTexture)

blitEncoder.endEncoding()

guard let computeEncoder
    = cb.makeComputeCommandEncoder() else { return }

computeEncoder.setComputePipelineState(self.compute
Pipeline)

// Bind both textures.

computeEncoder.setTexture(target, index: 0)

computeEncoder.setTexture(intermediateTexture,
index: 1)

// Bind settings data.

computeEncoder.setBytes(
    &self.settings,
    length: MemoryLayout<TwirlSettings>.size,
    index: 0
)

let workgroup = MTLSize(
    width: computePipeline.threadExecutionWidth,
    height: computePipeline.maxTotalThreadsPer
            Threadgroup
```

```
                          / computePipeline.threadExecutionWidth,
            depth: 1
        )

        let imageSize = MTLSize(
            width: target.width,
            height: target.height,
            depth: target.depth
        )

        computeEncoder.dispatchThreadgroups(
            divUp(imageSize, workgroup),
            threadsPerThreadgroup: workgroup
        )

        computeEncoder.endEncoding()
    }
}
```

Twirl Shader

In TwirlShader.metal, add the following code.

```
#include <metal_stdlib>
using namespace metal;

#include "./TwirlSettings.h"

kernel void twirlCS(
    texture2d<float, access::write> targetTexture
[[texture(0)]],
    texture2d<float, access::sample> srcTexture [[texture(1)]],
    uint2 gid [[thread_position_in_grid]],
```

```
    constant TwirlSettings* settings [[buffer(0)]]
) {
    // ...
}
```

Note that there are two texture bindings and the buffer binding for the settings.

To implement the twirl effect, you must compute the vector from the center for each pixel and rotate it (see Figure 12-2).

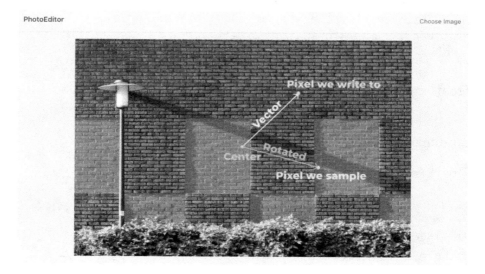

Figure 12-2. *Pixel displacement visualization*

Here's how to calculate the vector.

```
// UV coordinates of the current pixel.
float2 uv = float2(gid) / float2(targetTexture.get_width(),
targetTexture.get_height());

// Center of UV cooridnates.
float2 center = float2(0.5, 0.5);
```

```
// Here we make a vector from center to the pixel we process.
float2 vector = uv - center;
```

Next, you need to rotate the vector. To do so, let's construct a 2x2 rotation matrix for a 2D vector.

```
float twirlAngle = settings->angle.
```

```
// Rotation matrix.
float2x2 rotation = float2x2(
    metal::cos(twirlAngle), metal::sin(twirlAngle),
    -metal::sin(twirlAngle), metal::cos(twirlAngle)
);
```

```
float2 rotatedVector = vector * rotation;
```

After rotating the vector, you can now calculate the new UV coordinates it points to.

```
float2 rotatedUv = center + rotatedVector;
```

The following is the full version of the shader.

```
#include <metal_stdlib>
using namespace metal;

#include "./TwirlSettings.h"

kernel void twirlCS(
    texture2d<float, access::write> targetTexture
    [[texture(0)]],
    texture2d<float, access::sample> srcTexture [[texture(1)]],
    uint2 gid [[thread_position_in_grid]],
    constant TwirlSettings* settings [[buffer(0)]]
) {
```

```
// UV coordinates of the current pixel.
float2 uv = float2(gid) / float2(
    targetTexture.get_width(),
    targetTexture.get_height()
);

// Center of UV cooridnates.
float2 center = float2(0.5, 0.5);

// Here we make a vector from center to the pixel we
process.
float2 vector = uv - center;

float twirlAngle = settings->angle;

// Rotation matrix.
float2x2 rotation = float2x2(
    metal::cos(twirlAngle), metal::sin(twirlAngle),
    -metal::sin(twirlAngle), metal::cos(twirlAngle)
);

float2 rotatedVector = vector * rotation;

float2 rotatedUv = center + rotatedVector;

constexpr sampler linearSampler(
    mag_filter::linear, min_filter::linear
);

targetTexture.write(
    srcTexture.sample(linearSampler, rotatedUv),
    gid
);
}
```

Execute it. Figure 12-3 shows the result.

Figure 12-3. *Image, rotated by the compute shader*

The entire image was successfully rotated. However, only a portion of the image needs to be rotated for the twirl effect, which is why a radius parameter is needed.

To achieve this, you must scale down the twirl angle based on the distance from the center—a similar approach to what was used in the vignette shader. Let's use the smoothstep function to calculate this factor, ensuring a smooth result at the edges.

```
float angleFactor = 1.0 - smoothstep(
    0.0, 1.0, metal::length(vector) / settings->radius
);

// Apply the factor to the angle.
float twirlAngle = settings->angle * angleFactor;
```

Before examining the final result, let's consider the `angleFactor` value. Its output is as follows.

```
targetTexture.write(
    float4(angleFactor, angleFactor, angleFactor, 1.0), gid
);
```

Figure 12-4 shows the result. It should effectively confine the twirl effect to the white portion of the image.

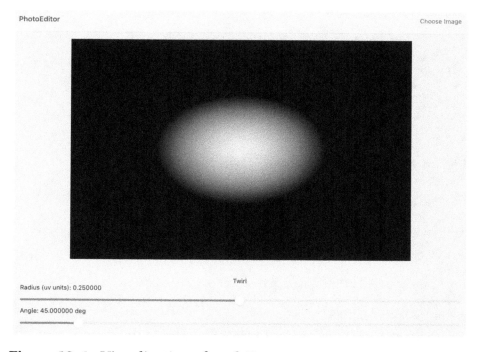

Figure 12-4. *Visualization of angleFactor*

Final Result

Executing the code produces a beautiful twirl effect, as shown in Figure 12-5.

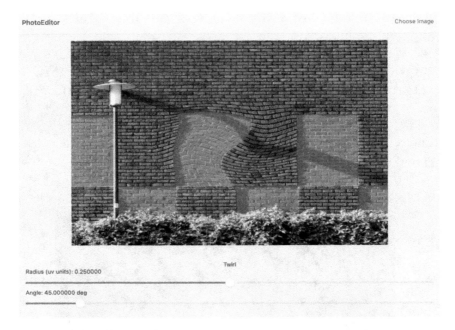

Figure 12-5. *Twirl displacement effect, applied to the image*

The following is the final version of the shader.

```
#include <metal_stdlib>
using namespace metal;

#include "./TwirlSettings.h"

kernel void twirlCS(
    texture2d<float, access::write> targetTexture
[[texture(0)]],
    texture2d<float, access::sample> srcTexture [[texture(1)]],
    uint2 gid [[thread_position_in_grid]],
    constant TwirlSettings* settings [[buffer(0)]]
) {
    // UV coordinates of the current pixel.
```

```
float2 uv = float2(gid) / float2(
    targetTexture.get_width(),
    targetTexture.get_height()
);

// Center of UV cooridnates.
float2 center = float2(0.5, 0.5);

// Here we make a vector from center to the pixel we
process.
float2 vector = uv - center;

float angleFactor = 1.0 - smoothstep(
    0.0, 1.0, metal::length(vector) / settings->radius
);

// Apply the factor to the angle.
float twirlAngle = settings->angle * angleFactor;

// Rotation matrix.
float2x2 rotation = float2x2(
    metal::cos(twirlAngle), metal::sin(twirlAngle),
    -metal::sin(twirlAngle), metal::cos(twirlAngle)
);

float2 rotatedVector = vector * rotation;

float2 rotatedUv = center + rotatedVector;

constexpr sampler linearSampler(
    mag_filter::linear,
    min_filter::linear
);
```

```
targetTexture.write(
    srcTexture.sample(linearSampler, rotatedUv),
    gid
);
}
```

Conclusion

This chapter explored displacement effects, specifically implementing a twirl effect. You learned to rotate pixels around a specific point and limit the effect within a particular radius.

As with any effect, the best way to understand it is to experiment. Try changing the radius and angle parameters and observe how they impact the result. You might also consider adding more parameters to customize the effect, such as an offset to move the center of the twirl.

PART III

Multilayer Rendering

CHAPTER 13

Introduction to Layer Composition

By the end of this chapter, you will have implemented a complete layer system in the photo editor, allowing for multiple images with different transformations and transparency levels to be composed into a final output. Figure 13-1 shows the expected result of this implementation.

Figure 13-1. *Final composed image with multiple layers and transformations*

© Bogdan Redkin and Victor Yaskevich 2024
B. Redkin and V. Yaskevich, *Master Photo and Video Editing with Metal*,
https://doi.org/10.1007/979-8-8688-0832-6_13

So far, you have only rendered opaque content from processing individual images with modified pixels. In this chapter, you implement a layer system in the photo editor. This system allows you to compose a final image from different images with applied transformations and transparency.

Layer composition with transparency is a fundamental feature; almost every graphic design application released in the last two decades supports it. You will implement transparency with a technique called **alpha blending**, which allows you to combine colors already in the frame buffer with partially transparent fragment colors, creating the illusion of transparent objects.

Alpha Compositing

Opacity

Many images and textures include a channel called the alpha channel. Alongside the red, green, and blue components of a color, the alpha component represents the color's **opacity**, which defines how much light is blocked by an object. The opposite of this property is **transparency**, which measures how much light passes through a surface.

Understanding Image Composition

Compositing is merging colors or elements from two or more images to generate the final output. This process often involves multiple steps, with each step merging a background and a foreground image. The result of each step then becomes the background image for the next step. Figure 13-2 illustrates this concept.

Figure 13-2. *The alpha compositing process with background and foreground blending*

When implementing alpha blending, the existing contents of the frame buffer are the background, and the current fragment serves as the foreground. If the alpha component of the fragment is 0 (indicating full transparency), the background remains unchanged. The fragment replaces the background if the alpha component is 1 (indicating opacity). Alpha values between 0 and 1 result in a blend of colors according to the opacity of the foreground.

Alpha Blending

Now that you understand compositing, let's discuss how the GPU implements transparency.

Alpha blending combines the previously rendered content with the current layer. These blending calculations are defined in the fragment shader function with arguments containing resources required for calculations.

The list of fragment function arguments includes the background texture, current texture, and opacity. After receiving these values, the color combination begins by fetching current pixel data from background and foreground textures and blending them using the equation $F * m + B(1 - m)$.

This equation is encoded inside the Mix function. If the Mix value is 1, the output is identical to the foreground value. If the value is 0, the output is identical to the background value. The closer the Mix value is to 0 or 1, the closer the output is to the corresponding input. The calculated color is then returned as a result texture. Figure 13-3 shows how this equation is applied to achieve the final blended color.

Background

Foreground

Mix value of 0.1

Mix value of 0.5

Mix value of 0.9

Figure 13-3.   *Color blending using the equation $F \times m + B(1 - m)$*

The result of the processed texture is used as a background for the next blending.

Implement Layers Composition

Let's open the starter project and examine the key layer storage and preparation components.

- **Layer** represents a single layer in the rendering tool. It includes properties such as transformation matrix, opacity, and surface.

  - Transform is a class that handles the transformation properties of a layer, such as scale, translation, and rotation, and generates the transformation matrix.

  - ContentLayerSurface manages the layer's content, such as the image or background texture.

  - Opacity determines the alpha channel for overlaying during the composition processing.

- LayerRenderingTool manages the rendering pipeline, processes each layer, and handles the blending and compositing of layers onto the target texture.

- PhotoEditorDataModel manages the layers and their properties through the FilterControlsView list responsible for submitting user-entered values to the currently selected layer. At the same time, it sends current data from the rendering tool to the UI when the chosen layer is updated.

Figure 13-4 provides a visual overview of how layers are managed and transformed within the rendering tool.

Figure 13-4. *A screenshot of the application demonstrates the managing layers and transformations*

Launch the starter project, add a new layer, and try to update transformations.

As you can see, the result of layer transformations causes a glitch in the background. This happens because there is no background texture to overlay the result of transformations.

Layer Transformations

Once the layer content is in its associated texture, you can use a rasterization pipeline. Each layer has transform data associated with it, which is passed to the vertex shader to position the layer texture.

Implementing Alpha Compositing

The first step for implementing alpha compositing is to create a white background texture to use as the initial background for the first layer in the stack.

To do so, update the LayerRenderingTool initialization with this code.

```
let whiteTexture: MTLTexture

init(device: MTLDevice) throws {
    self.whiteTexture = makeWhiteTexture(device: device)!
    // ...
}
```

Now, you need to set this texture as a background for the first layer in the rendering stack. Update the rendering pipeline configuration in the render(cb: MTLCommandBuffer, target: MTLTexture) method with the following code.

```
let isFirstLayer = layerIndex == 0

let bgTexture: MTLTexture

// Pick the background to draw on top of
if isFirstLayer {
    renderPass.colorAttachments[0].loadAction = .clear

    renderPass.colorAttachments[0].clearColor
        = MTLClearColor(
            red: 1.0, green: 1.0,
            blue: 1.0, alpha: 1.0
        )

    bgTexture = self.whiteTexture
```

```
} else {
    renderPass.colorAttachments[0].loadAction = .load

    bgTexture = target
}

if let encoder = cb.makeRenderCommandEncoder(descriptor:
renderPass)
{
    let pipeline = self.makeAlphaBlendingPipeline(device:
    device)
    encoder.setRenderPipelineState(pipeline)
    encoder.setViewport(viewport)
    var matrix: matrix_float4x4 = layer.transform.makeMatrix(
        width: target.width, height: target.height
    )
    var mixFactor: Float = layer.opacity
    encoder.setVertexBytes(&matrix, length: 4 * 4 * 4,
    index: 0)
    encoder.setFragmentTexture(layer.surface.target, index: 0)
    encoder.setFragmentTexture(bgTexture, index: 1)
    encoder.setFragmentBytes(&mixFactor, length: 4, index: 0)
    encoder.drawPrimitives(
        type: .triangle, vertexStart: 0, vertexCount: 6
    )
    encoder.endEncoding()
}
```

This code sets up the background texture for the first rendered layer and then submits bgTexture to the fragment shader function along with mixFactor from the opacity property of the current rendered layer. However, the fragment shader function doesn't support these arguments yet. Let's update it!

Update the Pipeline to Support Blending

Open the LayerShader.metal file, and create a new fragment shader that handles blending.

```
fragment float4 layerNormalBlendFS(
    VertexOutput in [[stage_in]],
    texture2d<float> texture [[texture(0)]],
    texture2d<float> bg [[texture(1)]],
    constant float& opacity [[ buffer(0) ]]
) {
    constexpr sampler textureSampler(
        mag_filter::linear,
        min_filter::linear
    );
    float4 layerColor = texture.sample(textureSampler, in.uv);
    // BG color always has alpha = 1.0
    float3 bgColor = bg.sample(textureSampler, in.bgUv).rgb;
    float3 blended = layerColor.rgb;
    float alpha = layerColor.a * opacity;
    float3 output = mix(bgColor, blended, alpha);
    return float4(output, 1.0);
}
```

Update the makeAlphaBlendingPipeline method to use this new fragment shader.

```
let fragmentFunction = library.makeFunction(
    name: "layerNormalBlendFS"
)
```

Build and run the sample project. Try to add a few new layers with updated opacity values. Figure 13-5 demonstrates the result after adding layers with various opacities.

Figure 13-5. *Result of adding layers with different opacity values*

Final Result

Let's make one last update for testing purposes. Open the PhotoEditorView.swift file, and update the rendering tool initialization to this code.

```
self.renderingTool = layerRenderingToolWithTestData(device:
device)
```

It creates the rendering tool with predefined layers and complex overlay and layer composition.

Build and run your project. Figure 13-6 shows the final rendering result with these predefined settings.

Figure 13-6. *Final rendering result with predefined layers and compositions*

Feel free to experiment with predefined opacity and transformations of layers.

Conclusion

In this chapter, you learned how to implement a layer system for the photo editor, enabling the composition of final images from multiple transformed and transparent images. You implemented transparency with alpha blending by using fragment shaders to blend colors from the frame buffer with partially transparent fragments, employing the equation $F \times m + B(1 - m)$.

The next chapter continues exploring blending with more complex blend modes.

CHAPTER 14

Blend Modes

The previous chapter introduced layer composition and implemented alpha blending to create transparent layers. This chapter explores additional blend modes that are essential for various artistic effects in graphic design based on image composition.

Blend Modes Overview

Layer blending is a process that determines how to mix the pixel colors of different images when layering one on top of another.

Let's open the starter project and look at the new and updated components involved in layer blending.

BlendMode is an enum that enumerates the various blend modes available in the photo editor. Each blend mode corresponds to a specific way of combining the colors of the top layer with the background layer.

```
enum BlendMode: String, CaseIterable {
    case normal
    case multiply
    // ...
}
```

The Layer class has been updated with a new property, blendMode, that stores the current selected blend mode.

© Bogdan Redkin and Victor Yaskevich 2024
B. Redkin and V. Yaskevich, *Master Photo and Video Editing with Metal*,
https://doi.org/10.1007/979-8-8688-0832-6_14

BlendingPipelines is responsible for initializing and storing the pipelines for each blend mode, which are used during rendering.

```
struct BlendingPipelines {
    let normal: MTLRenderPipelineState

    let multiply: MTLRenderPipelineState

    // ...

    init(device: MTLDevice) {
        self.normal = makeBlendingPipeline(
            device: device, fragmentName: "layerNormalBlendFS"
        )

        self.multiply = makeBlendingPipeline(
            device: device, fragmentName: "layerMultiply
            BlendFS"
        )

        // ... blending pipelines initializing
    }

    func getPipeline(
        for blendMode: BlendMode
    ) -> MTLRenderPipelineState {
        // ... return configured blending pipeline
    }
}
```

LayerRenderingTool has been updated to use the appropriate pipeline for each layer based on its blend mode.

```
final class LayerRenderingTool: RenderingTool {
    private let blendingPipelines: BlendingPipelines

    // ...
```

```
func render(cb: MTLCommandBuffer, target: MTLTexture) {
    // ...

    // The render function iterates through each layer and
    // selects the appropriate render pipeline based on the
    // layer's blend mode
    let pipeline = self.blendingPipelines.getPipeline(
        for: layer.blendMode
    )

    encoder.setRenderPipelineState(pipeline)

    // ...
}
}
```

Implementing Blend Modes

Since the starter project already includes the required configurations, you can begin implementing blend modes. The "required configurations" are predefined fragment function names stored in BlendingPipelines. To add a new blend mode, you only need to insert a corresponding fragment function in the LayerShader.metal file.

Multiply

To add multiply blending support, insert the following code into the LayerShader.metal file.

```
fragment float4 layerMultiplyBlendFS(
    VertexOutput in [[stage_in]],
    texture2d<float> texture [[texture(0)]],
```

```
    texture2d<float> bg [[texture(1)]],
    constant float& opacity [[ buffer(0) ]]
) {
    constexpr sampler textureSampler(
        mag_filter::linear, min_filter::linear
    );

    float4 layerColor = texture.sample(textureSampler, in.uv);

    // BG color always has alpha = 1.0
    float3 bgColor = bg.sample(textureSampler, in.bgUv).rgb;

    float3 blended = bgColor * layerColor.rgb;

    return fragmentBlendingOutput(
        blended, bgColor, layerColor, opacity
    );
}
```

Build and run the updated example project, then select image layer 1 in the list of layers on the left side of the user interface. After that, select the multiply blend mode in the blending mode drop-down menu on the right side of the user interface, as shown in Figure 14-1.

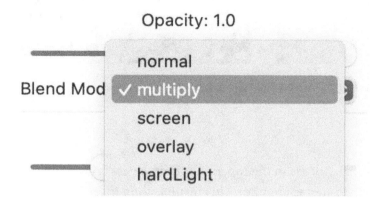

Figure 14-1. *The user interface for blend mode selection*

After this manipulation, the rendering result should look darker because the multiply blend mode multiplies the top layer color over the bottom layer, so the result color is always smaller than the background and source colors. A smaller color value means a darker color value.

Multiply blend mode can be represented as an equation (see Figure 14-2).

$$B(C_{dst}, C_{src}) = C_{dst} \times C_{src}$$

Figure 14-2. *The equation representing the multiply blend mode*

The rendering result is shown in Figure 14-3.

Figure 14-3. The rendering result of the multiply blend mode

Screen

Color information from the top and bottom layers is inverted and multiplied against each other. This result is then inverted again. This produces a visual result that is the opposite of the multiply blending mode and gives a brighter image.

The inversion in color blending is achieved by subtracting the color value from white (1.0). Figure 14-4 features the equation describing the calculations.

$$B(C_{dst}, C_{src}) = 1 - ((1 - C_{dst}) * (1 - C_{src}))$$

Figure 14-4. The equation describing the calculation for the screen blend mode

The following is the equation implementation in the fragment function.

```
fragment float4 layerScreenBlendFS(
    VertexOutput in [[stage_in]],
    texture2d<float> texture [[texture(0)]],
    texture2d<float> bg [[texture(1)]],
    constant float& opacity [[ buffer(0) ]]
) {
```

```
constexpr sampler textureSampler(
    mag_filter::linear, min_filter::linear
);

float4 layerColor = texture.sample(textureSampler, in.uv);

// BG color always has alpha = 1.0
float3 bgColor = bg.sample(textureSampler, in.bgUv).rgb;
float3 white = float3(1.0);

float3 blended
    = white - ((white - layerColor.rgb) *
      (white - bgColor));

return fragmentBlendingOutput(
    blended, bgColor, layerColor, opacity
);
}
```

As a result, this blending always produces a brighter image than the source image, as shown in Figure 14-5.

Figure 14-5. *Overlay using the screen blend mode*

Overlay

An **overlay** combines **multiply** and **screen** blend modes. Where the background layer (C_{dst}) is light, the top layer (C_{src}) becomes lighter; where the base layer is dark, the top becomes darker; where the base layer is mid-gray, the top is unaffected. An overlay with the same picture looks like an S-curve. Figure 14-6 features the equation representing the overlay blend mode.

$$B(C_{dst}, C_{src}) = \begin{cases} 2 * C_{dst} * C_{src} & \text{if } C_{dst} < 0.5 \\ 1 - 2 * ((1 - C_{dst}) * (1 - C_{src})) & \text{otherwise} \end{cases}$$

Figure 14-6. *The equation representing overlay blend mode*

The following is the fragment function that implemented this algorithm.

```
fragment float4 layerOverlayBlendFS(
    VertexOutput in [[stage_in]],
    texture2d<float> texture [[texture(0)]],
    texture2d<float> bg [[texture(1)]],
    constant float& opacity [[ buffer(0) ]]
) {
    constexpr sampler textureSampler(
        mag_filter::linear, min_filter::linear
    );

    float4 layerColor = texture.sample(textureSampler, in.uv);

    // BG color always has alpha = 1.0
    float3 bgColor = bg.sample(textureSampler, in.bgUv).rgb;

    float3 blended = mix(
        2.0 * bgColor * layerColor.rgb,
        1.0 - 2.0 * (1.0 - bgColor) * (1.0 - layerColor.rgb),
```

```
        step(0.5, bgColor)
    );

    return fragmentBlendingOutput(
        blended, bgColor, layerColor, opacity
    );
}
```

Figure 14-7 shows the processing result using the overlay blend mode.

Figure 14-7. *The processing result using the overlay blend mode*

As you can see in the processing result, the grayscale values in the top layer have no effect, but dark colors multiply colors, and bright colors lighten the colors.

Hard Light

The **hard light** blend mode is also a combination of multiply and screen. Hard light affects the blend layer's relationship to the base layer in the same way overlay affects the base layer's relationship to the blend layer. Figure 14-8 shows the equation representing hard light blend mode.

$$B(C_{dst}, C_{src}) = \begin{cases} 2 * C_{dst} * C_{src} & \text{if } C_{src} < 0.5 \\ 1 - 2 * ((1 - C_{dst}) * (1 - C_{src})) & \text{otherwise} \end{cases}$$

Figure 14-8. *Equation representing hard light blend mode*

The inverse relationship between overlay and hard light makes them **commuted blend modes**.

```
fragment float4 layerHardLightBlendFS(
    VertexOutput in [[stage_in]],
    texture2d<float> texture [[texture(0)]],
    texture2d<float> bg [[texture(1)]],
    constant float& opacity [[ buffer(0) ]]
) {
    constexpr sampler textureSampler(
        mag_filter::linear, min_filter::linear
    );

    float4 layerColor = texture.sample(textureSampler, in.uv);

    // BG color always has alpha = 1.0
    float3 bgColor = bg.sample(textureSampler, in.bgUv).rgb;

    float3 blended = mix(
        2.0 * layerColor.rgb * bgColor,
        1.0 - 2.0 * (1.0 - bgColor) * (1.0 - layerColor.rgb),
        step(0.5, layerColor.rgb)
    );

    return fragmentBlendingOutput(
        blended, bgColor, layerColor, opacity
    );
}
```

Figure 14-9 shows the processing result of the hard light blend mode.

***Figure 14-9.** The processing result of the hard light blend mode*

The blended result differs due to the order of operations, resulting in an image with darker or brighter colors but less contrast.

Soft Light

The **soft light** blend mode is closely related to overlay and is only similar to hard light by name. Applying pure black or white does not result in pure black or white. Unlike overlay, soft light is applied with a different curve to blend the color information, which results in a less contrasted image. Figures 14-10 and 14-11 show the calculations for a soft light blend mode.

$$\text{g} = \begin{cases} ((16 * C_{dst} - 12) * C_{dst} + 4) * C_{dst} & \text{if } C_{dst} \leqslant 0.25 \\ \sqrt{C_{dst}} & \text{otherwise} \end{cases}$$

***Figure 14-10.** The first part of calculations for soft light blend mode*

$$B(C_{dst}, C_{src}) = \begin{cases} C_{dst} - (1 - 2 * C_{src}) * C_{dst} * (1.0 - C_{dst}) & \text{if } C_{src} \leqslant 0.5 \\ C_{dst} + (2 * C_{src} - 1) * (\text{g} - C_{dst}) & \text{otherwise} \end{cases}$$

***Figure 14-11.** The second part of the calculations the soft light blend mode*

It is still a linear interpolation between 3 images for $C_{src} = (0,0.5,1)$. But now, the image for $C_{src} = 1$ is not $g = 0.5$, but the result of a tonal curve that differs from the curve of $g = 0.5$ for small values of C_{src}: while gamma correction with $g = 0.5$ may increase the value of C_{src} many times, this new curve limits the increase of C_{src} by coefficient 4.

```
fragment float4 layerSoftLightBlendFS(
    VertexOutput in [[stage_in]],
    texture2d<float> texture [[texture(0)]],
    texture2d<float> bg [[texture(1)]],
    constant float& opacity [[ buffer(0) ]]
) {
    constexpr sampler textureSampler(
        mag_filter::linear, min_filter::linear
    );

    float4 layerColor = texture.sample(textureSampler, in.uv);

    // BG color always has alpha = 1.0
    float3 bgColor = bg.sample(textureSampler, in.bgUv).rgb;

    float3 g = mix(
        ((16.0 * bgColor - 12.0) * bgColor + 4) * bgColor,
        sqrt(bgColor),
        step(0.25, bgColor)
    );

    float3 blended = mix(
        bgColor - (1.0 - 2.0 * layerColor.rgb)
                                    * bgColor * (1.0 - bgColor),
        bgColor + (2.0 * layerColor.rgb - 1.0) * (g - bgColor),
        step(0.5, layerColor.rgb)
    );
```

```
return fragmentBlendingOutput(
    blended, bgColor, layerColor, opacity
);
}
```

Figure 14-12 shows the processing result of the overlay with soft light blend mode.

Figure 14-12. *The processing result of the overlay with soft light blend mode*

Color Burn

The **color burn** mode divides the inverted bottom layer by the top layer and then inverts the result. This darkens the top layer, increasing the contrast to reflect the color of the bottom layer. The darker the bottom layer, the more its color is used. Blending with white produces no difference. When the top layer contains a homogeneous color, this effect is equivalent to changing the black point to the inverted color.

The formula is given in Figure 14-13.

$$B(Cdst, Csrc) = 1 - min(1, (1 - Cdst)/Csrc)$$

Figure 14-13. *The formula of calculations for color burn blend mode*

It transforms to the fragment function as follows.

```
fragment float4 layerColorBurnBlendFS(
    VertexOutput in [[stage_in]],
    texture2d<float> texture [[texture(0)]],
    texture2d<float> bg [[texture(1)]],
    constant float& opacity [[ buffer(0) ]]
) {
    constexpr sampler textureSampler(
        mag_filter::linear, min_filter::linear
    );

    float4 layerColor = texture.sample(textureSampler, in.uv);

    // BG color always has alpha = 1.0
    float3 bgColor = bg.sample(textureSampler, in.bgUv).rgb;

    float3 blended
            = 1.0 - min(1.0, (1.0 - bgColor) / layerColor.rgb);

    return fragmentBlendingOutput(
        blended, bgColor, layerColor, opacity
    );
}
```

The result of blending processing is shown in Figure 14-14.

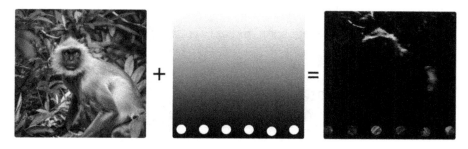

Figure 14-14. *The processing result of overlay using the color burn blend mode*

Darken

A **darken** blend mode only creates a pixel that retains the smallest components of the foreground and background pixels. Figure 14-15 presents the calculation of a darken blend mode.

$$B(C_{dst}, C_{src}) = min(C_{dst}, C_{src})$$

Figure 14-15. *Calculating the darken blend mode*

```
fragment float4 layerDarkenBlendFS(
    VertexOutput in [[stage_in]],
    texture2d<float> texture [[texture(0)]],
    texture2d<float> bg [[texture(1)]],
    constant float& opacity [[ buffer(0) ]]
) {
    constexpr sampler textureSampler(
        mag_filter::linear, min_filter::linear
    );

    float4 layerColor = texture.sample(textureSampler, in.uv);
```

```
// BG color always has alpha = 1.0
float3 bgColor = bg.sample(textureSampler, in.bgUv).rgb;

float3 blended = min(bgColor, layerColor.rgb);

return fragmentBlendingOutput(
    blended, bgColor, layerColor, opacity
);
}
```

The result of blending processing is shown in Figure 14-16.

Figure 14-16. *The processing result of overlay using the darken blend mode*

Lighten

A **lighten** blend mode keeps the maximum color value between the top and bottom layers. Figure 14-17 presents the calculation for the lighten blend mode.

$$B(C_{dst}, C_{src}) = max(C_{dst}, C_{src})$$

Figure 14-17. *The calculation for the lighten blend mode*

```
fragment float4 layerLightenBlendFS(
    VertexOutput in [[stage_in]],
```

```
    texture2d<float> texture [[texture(0)]],
    texture2d<float> bg [[texture(1)]],
    constant float& opacity [[ buffer(0) ]]
) {
    constexpr sampler textureSampler(
        mag_filter::linear, min_filter::linear
    );

    float4 layerColor = texture.sample(textureSampler, in.uv);

    // BG color always has alpha = 1.0
    float3 bgColor = bg.sample(textureSampler, in.bgUv).rgb;

    float3 blended = max(bgColor, layerColor.rgb);

    return fragmentBlendingOutput(
        blended, bgColor, layerColor, opacity
    );
}
```

The result of blending processing is illustrated in Figure 14-18.

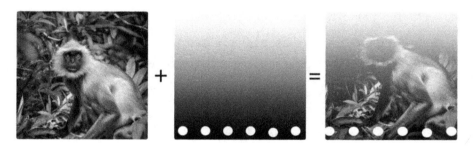

Figure 14-18.   *The rendering result of image overlay using the lighten blend mode*

Difference

The **difference** blend mode subtracts the top layer color from the bottom layer, but takes the absolute value of the result (negative values become positive). It is represented as an equation in Figure 14-19.

$$B(C_{dst}, C_{src}) = |C_{dst} - C_{src}|$$

Figure 14-19. *The equation for the difference blend mode*

```
fragment float4 layerDifferenceBlendFS(
    VertexOutput in [[stage_in]],
    texture2d<float> texture [[texture(0)]],
    texture2d<float> bg [[texture(1)]],
    constant float& opacity [[ buffer(0) ]]
) {
    constexpr sampler textureSampler(
        mag_filter::linear, min_filter::linear
    );

    float4 layerColor = texture.sample(textureSampler, in.uv);

    // BG color always has alpha = 1.0
    float3 bgColor = bg.sample(textureSampler, in.bgUv).rgb;

    float3 blended = abs(bgColor - layerColor.rgb);

    return fragmentBlendingOutput(
        blended, bgColor, layerColor, opacity
    );
}
```

The result of blending processing is shown in Figure 14-20.

Figure 14-20. *The rendering result of difference blend mode*

Subtract

The **subtract** blend mode subtracts the top layer color from the bottom layer. The result can give colors below 0, in which case the result is clamped/clipped. Figure 14-21 is the formula for subtract blend mode.

$$B(C_{dst}, C_{src}) = C_{dst} - C_{src}$$

Figure 14-21. *The calculation of subtract blend mode*

```
fragment float4 layerSubtractBlendFS(
    VertexOutput in [[stage_in]],
    texture2d<float> texture [[texture(0)]],
    texture2d<float> bg [[texture(1)]],
    constant float& opacity [[ buffer(0) ]]
) {
    constexpr sampler textureSampler(
        mag_filter::linear, min_filter::linear
    );

    float4 layerColor = texture.sample(textureSampler, in.uv);

    // BG color always has alpha = 1.0
    float3 bgColor = bg.sample(textureSampler, in.bgUv).rgb;
```

```
float3 blended = float3(bgColor - layerColor.rgb);

return fragmentBlendingOutput(
    blended, bgColor, layerColor, opacity
);
}
```

The result of blending processing is shown in Figure 14-22.

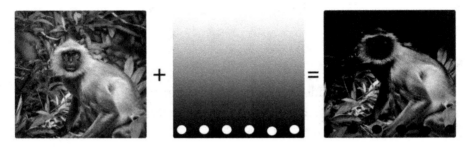

Figure 14-22. *The result of subtracting blending processing*

Conclusion

This chapter explored various blend modes and their implementation in Metal. Each blend mode offers unique ways to combine the colors of different layers, providing a wide range of artistic effects. By understanding these blend modes and what kind of blending suits specific tasks, you can achieve more complex and visually appealing compositions in your photo and video editing projects.

The next chapter continues improving the sample photo editing app by adding support for applying layer-specific effects.

CHAPTER 15

Layer Effects

Part III of this book worked with compute shaders to create visual effects by modifying image pixels. This chapter integrates these effects into the layer composition pipeline. To accomplish this, you will use a separate texture for each layer, referred to as a **layer surface**. Then, you render these layer surfaces and blend them together using the blending mechanism in the layer composition pipeline. These steps are visualized in Figure 15-1.

© Bogdan Redkin and Victor Yaskevich 2024
B. Redkin and V. Yaskevich, *Master Photo and Video Editing with Metal*,
https://doi.org/10.1007/979-8-8688-0832-6_15

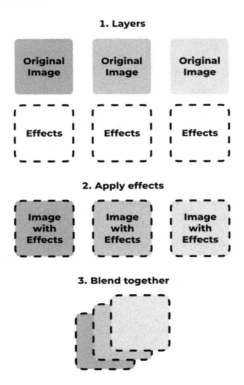

Figure 15-1. *Steps to blend layers with effects*

Implementation

First, let's define a class to store the source image and the list of effects applied to it.

This class has two textures. One is the source image the user selects, which is never modified. The second texture created is the render target. In each render loop iteration, you initialize that texture with source pixels and then apply effects. After applying these effects, you have the final image, which you export from the class to be accessible by the blending mechanism implemented in previous chapters.

Note how the render target texture is created. It must have the proper usage flags to allow read and write operations in compute shaders.

In the render method, we encode commands to copy the source texture content into the render target. Then, we iterate through the enabled effects and encode their render commands.

```
// Utility wrapper, that has the flag whether the effect is
enabled.
final class TogglableEffect {
    let effect: EffectPass
    var isEnabled: Bool = false

    init(effect: EffectPass) {
        self.effect = effect
    }
}

final class ContentLayerSurface {
    let source: MTLTexture

    // Our render target texture
    var texture: MTLTexture

    var effects: [TogglableEffect]

    init(device: MTLDevice, sourceImage: URL) throws {
        self.source = try MTKTextureLoader(device: device)
            .newTexture(
                URL: sourceImage,
                options: [
                    .textureUsage: MTLTextureUsage.shaderRead
                    .rawValue,
                    .textureStorageMode: MTLStorageMode.private
                    .rawValue
                ]
            )
```

```swift
let targetDesc = MTLTextureDescriptor.
                  texture2DDescriptor(
    pixelFormat: self.source.pixelFormat,
    width: self.source.width,
    height: self.source.height,
    mipmapped: false
)

targetDesc.usage = [.shaderRead, .renderTarget,
                    .shaderWrite]
targetDesc.storageMode  = .private

self.texture = device.makeTexture(descriptor:
                targetDesc)!

var availableEffects: [any EffectPass] = []
do {
    availableEffects = [
        // Here we put effects we've created.
        // ...
    ]
} catch {
    print("error of effects initalizing: \(error)")
}

self.effects = availableEffects.map {
    TogglableEffect(effect: $0) }
}

func render(cb: MTLCommandBuffer) {
    // Copy source image to the render target
    if let blitEncoder = cb.makeBlitCommandEncoder() {
```

```
        blitEncoder.copy(from: self.source, to: self.
        texture)
        blitEncoder.endEncoding()
    }

    let enabledEffects = self.effects.filter({ $0.isEnabled })

    for effect in enabledEffects {
        effect.effect.writeCommands(
            cb: cb, target: self.texture
        )
    }
    }
}
```

Integrating into Layers Pipeline

Since the layer's interface did not change much, integrating it into the blending mechanism is very simple.

The only thing you need to add is to render the layers before blending them. To do that, just iterate through the list of layers and call the render method before encoding the blending commands.

```
// Render content layers
for layer in self.layers {
    layer.surface.render(cb: cb)
}

// Our blending render loop code
// ...
```

Results

Let's run it. The results are shown in Figure 15-2.

Figure 15-2. *Two layers with effects blended together*

Figure 15-3 shows it with some blend mode.

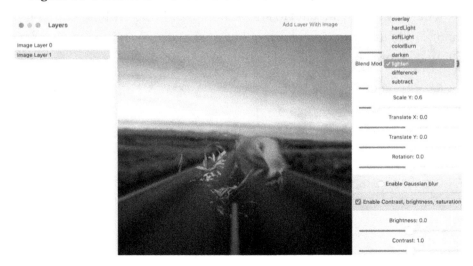

Figure 15-3. *Two layers with effects blended together with lighten blend mode*

256

Conclusion

This chapter connected the effects implemented in the previous chapter to the layer composition pipeline. By combining visual effects created by compute shaders with the blending pipeline, which is implemented using the classic graphics pipeline with vertex and fragment shaders, you learned how different rendering approaches can be used together to achieve greater flexibility and creativity in rendering techniques.

PART IV

Video Editing with Metal

CHAPTER 16

Video Editing with Metal

So far, you've been working only with static images, where each source texture remains the same throughout the whole processing pipeline.

This chapter explains video processing and how to manage a continuous stream of new frames, applying transformations and effects in real time. This chapter is a significant step forward in your Metal journey, as mastering video editing unlocks numerous potential features for your app.

Video Processing Pipeline Overview

The video-editing workflow in Metal includes two stages.

- The **AVFoundation stage** is responsible for customizing the processing of each frame of the video. During this stage, each frame is converted to CVPixelBuffer and then to MTLTexture.

- In the **Metal processing stage**, the texture from the previous step is processed. This stage could include a complex sequence of GPU processing events, but

© Bogdan Redkin and Victor Yaskevich 2024
B. Redkin and V. Yaskevich, *Master Photo and Video Editing with Metal*,
https://doi.org/10.1007/979-8-8688-0832-6_16

this chapter uses a compute pipeline for applying effects. The result of this processing is converted back to `CVPixelBuffer` and submitted as a new frame for the video.

Customizing Video Processing with AVFoundation

The **AVFoundation** framework provides a feature-rich set of classes for working with media on iOS and macOS. The following is an overview of the components and their roles in video processing.

- `AVAsset` represents the media asset; our example uses it as a video data source. Assets also could include multiple audio and video tracks.

- `AVPlayerItem` models the timing and presentation state of AVAsset. It manages the current state of the asset and controls playback.

- `AVVideoComposition` specifies how video frames should be processed and combined. It supports a custom compositor class by defining your own implementation of the `AVVideoCompositing` protocol. This is the step where all video processing occurs.

- `AVPlayer` plays the media managed by `AVPlayerItem`, handling the playback of the processed video.

Figure 16-1 represents how a video is prepared and played.

Figure 16-1. *Overview of video preparation and playback with AVFoundation and AVPlayer*

Custom Video Composition Workflow

AVVideoComposition allows for the customization of the video processing workflow by supporting the definition of your own custom compositor that implements the AVVideoCompositing protocol. It also contains a list of instructions defining how video frames should be processed during specific time ranges.

- AVVideoCompositing allows you to define your own custom video compositor that controls how the video frame should be prepared to render, how the video frame should be rendered, and what kind of input and output pixel buffer attributes should be specified.

- AVVideoCompositionRenderContext provides information about the rendering environment, including the destination size and pixel format.

- AVAsynchronousVideoCompositionRequest handles requests to compose video frames asynchronously, providing access to the video frame and composition instructions.

- AVVideoCompositionInstruction provides instructions for a specific time range on how the video frames should be composed.

Figure 16-2 illustrates the custom video composition workflow, showing the interaction between these components.

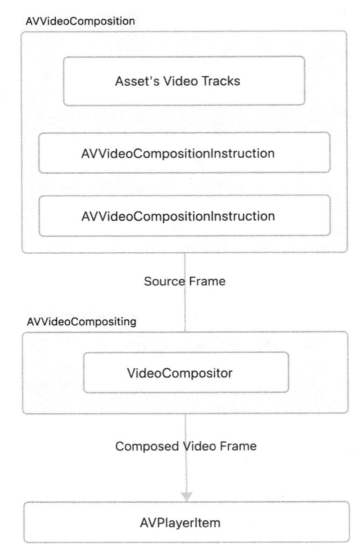

Figure 16-2. *Workflow of custom video composition using AVFoundation components*

Before proceeding to the next stage, where processing with Metal became involved, let's look at the starter project and update it with the implementation of AVVideoComposition with a custom compositor.

The Starter Project

To gradually increase the architecture complexity according to your progress with a new type of processing content, this chapter doesn't use LayerRenderingPipeline. You start with the basic image editing and effects application.

The starter project already includes implementing three main classes used during the video processing pipeline. The following describes their responsibilities.

- The VideoComposition actor and the VideoCompositor class are responsible for handling the AVAsynchronous VideoCompositionRequest request and executing an instruction with the current source frame pixel buffer and destination pixel buffer.

- VideoCompositionInstruction is responsible for processing pixel buffers and calling VideoRenderingTool for GPU processing.

- VideoRenderingTool is responsible for GPU processing and storing all the properties of current applied effects.

Figure 16-3 overviews these classes and their responsibilities.

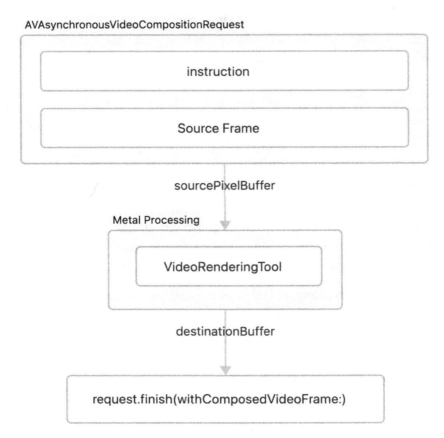

Figure 16-3. *Overview of custom classes involved in the video processing pipeline*

Create a Video Composition

Since all custom classes already have basic initialization methods, you can easily create them and provide all the necessary data from the selected asset.

Update the setAsset function in the VideoEditorView.swift file with the following code.

```
func setAsset(_ asset: AVURLAsset) {
    Task.init {
        do {
            let renderingTool = try VideoRenderingTool(device:
                            self.device)
            self.renderingTool = renderingTool
            let src = try await VideoComposition(renderingTool:
                    renderingTool, asset: asset)
            let videoComposition = await src.videoComposition

            let playerItem = AVPlayerItem(asset: asset)
            playerItem.videoComposition = videoComposition.
            copy() as? AVVideoComposition

            await MainActor.run {
                self.videoPlayer = AVPlayer(playerItem:
                                playerItem)
                self.videoPlayer?.play()
            }
        } catch {
            print("texture loading error: \\(error)")
        }
    }
}
```

After the instance of AVVideoComposition is created, it is used as a videoComposition property for AVPlayerItem, which means that every frame of the playing video is processed through the VideoCompositor because this class is used as a customCompositorClass property of this video composition.

Next, grab the current video frame and pass it along to compositionRequest as the composed video frame result.

```
func startRequest(_ asyncVideoCompositionRequest:
AVAsynchronousVideoCompositionRequest) {
    guard
        let sourceFrame = asyncVideoCompositionRequest.
                          sourceFrame(byTrackID:
                          asyncVideoCompositionRequest.
                          sourceTrackIDs[0].int32Value)
    else {
        asyncVideoCompositionRequest.finish(with: NSError
        (domain: "incorrect instruction", code: 0))
        return
    }

    asyncVideoCompositionRequest.finish(withComposedVideoFrame:
    sourceFrame)
}
```

Build and run your project. Figure 16-4 shows the result of implementing the video composition with a custom compositor.

Figure 16-4. *Result of basic video composition using a custom compositor*

With these changes, you have implemented a basic video composition with a custom video compositor class and composition request handling. The next step is to process the sourceFrame with Metal effects.

Processing Video Frames with Metal

Figure 16-5 represents the processTexture function, which processes the current frame of the video and returns it as a CGI image.

processTexture(from: completionHandler:)

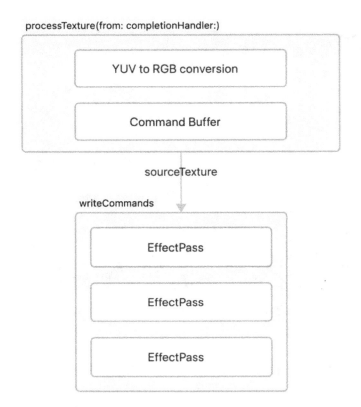

Figure 16-5. *Steps involved in processing a video frame with Metal*

Video frame processing starts with YUV to RGB color conversion. This conversion is required because the pixel format of `CVPixelBuffer` returned from the composition request is Y'CbCr. The YCbCr format, or YUV, is commonly used in video encoding.

YUVColorConversion

The YUV color space is used in video encoding because it separates luminance (Y) from chrominance (U and V), allowing for more efficient compression and better handling of color information in varying lighting conditions. This separation takes advantage of the human eye's ability to detect changes in brightness more easily than color changes, leading to a better overall image quality.

To convert YUV to RGB, perform the following steps.

1. **Extract Y, U, and V components.** Each pixel in the YUV format has a Y (luminance) value and two chrominance values (U and V).

2. **Apply color conversion matrix.** Use the standard YUV to RGB conversion formulas to compute the RGB values for each pixel.

Figure 16-6 is an example of intermediate textures showing luminance and chrominance values used in the conversion function.

Figure 16-6. *Intermediate textures showing luminance and chrominance values during YUV to RGB conversion*

In `VideoRenderingTool`, the `yuvConversionEffect` automatically handles this conversion. All you need to do is process the initial `sourceBuffer` property through `yuvConversionEffect`.

Here's how to update the `VideoRenderingTool` for YUV to RGB conversion.

```
func processTexure(from sourcePixelBuffer: CVPixelBuffer,
completionHandler: @escaping (CGImage?) -> Void) {
    guard
        let commandBuffer = commandQueue.makeCommandBuffer(),
        let sourceTexture = yuvConversionEffect.
        convertedTexture(cb: commandBuffer, from:
        sourcePixelBuffer)
    else { return }

    effects
        .filter { $0.isEnabled }
        .compactMap { $0.effect }
        .forEach {
            $0.writeCommands(cb: commandBuffer,
                            target: sourceTexture.texture)
        }

    commandBuffer.addCompletedHandler { _ in
        completionHandler(sourceTexture.texture.toImage())
    }

    commandBuffer.commit()
}
```

The conversion steps and intermediate textures are provided here to help you better understand the video processing pipeline. `yuvConversionEffect` is applied automatically, so you only need to pass the initial `sourceBuffer` property to it.

Handling Processed Frames

After processing VideoRenderingTool, the VideoCompositionInstruction class fills the destination buffer with the processed pixels.

Update the processPixelBuffer function inside the VideoCompositionInstruction class with the following code.

```
func processPixelBuffer(sourcePixelBuffer: CVPixelBuffer,
destinationBuffer: CVPixelBuffer, time: CMTime, finish:
@escaping (CVPixelBuffer) -> Void) {
    CVPixelBufferLockBaseAddress(sourcePixelBuffer, .readOnly)
    CVPixelBufferLockBaseAddress(destinationBuffer,
    CVPixelBufferLockFlags(rawValue: 0))

    renderingTool.processTexure(from: sourcePixelBuffer) {
    resultImage in
        guard let resultImage else {
            print("error obtaining cg image")
            finish(sourcePixelBuffer)
            return
        }

        let context = CGContext(data: CVPixelBufferGetBaseAdd
        ress(destinationBuffer),
                                width: resultImage.width,
                                height: resultImage.height,
                                bitsPerComponent:
                                resultImage.bitsPerComponent,
                                bytesPerRow: resultImage.
                                bytesPerRow,
                                space: resultImage.colorSpace!,
                                bitmapInfo: resultImage.
                                bitmapInfo.rawValue)
```

```
        context?.draw(resultImage, in: CGRect(origin: .zero,
        size: CGSize(width: resultImage.width, height:
        resultImage.height)), byTiling: false)
        CATransaction.flush()

        CVPixelBufferUnlockBaseAddress(destinationBuffer,
        CVPixelBufferLockFlags(rawValue: 0))
        CVPixelBufferUnlockBaseAddress(sourcePixelBuffer,
        .readOnly)

        finish(destinationBuffer)
    }
}
```

This function locks the base address of the source and destination pixel buffers, processes the texture using the rendering tool, and draws the resulting image into the destination buffer.

Next, update the VideoComposition actor's initialization with the following code.

```
init(renderingTool: VideoRenderingTool, asset: AVAsset) async
throws {
    ...
    self.videoComposition.instructions = [VideoCompositio
    nInstruction(renderingTool: renderingTool, timeRange:
    CMTimeRange(start: .zero, duration: CMTime(value: .max,
    timescale: 48000)))]
}
```

This code adds a composition instruction to cover the entire range of the source video.

Finally, the startRequest function from the composition request is where all the magic happens.

```
func startRequest(_ asyncVideoCompositionRequest:
AVAsynchronousVideoCompositionRequest) {
    guard
        let instruction = asyncVideoCompositionRequest.
         videoCompositionInstruction as? VideoComposition
         Instruction,
        let sourceFrame = asyncVideoCompositionRequest.
        sourceFrame(byTrackID: asyncVideoCompositionRequest.
        sourceTrackIDs[0].int32Value),
        let destinationBuffer = self.renderContext?.
        newPixelBuffer()
    else {
        asyncVideoCompositionRequest.finish(with: NSError
        (domain: "incorrect instruction", code: 0))
        return
    }

    let time = asyncVideoCompositionRequest.compositionTime

    instruction.processPixelBuffer(sourcePixelBuffer:
    sourceFrame, destinationBuffer: destinationBuffer, time:
    time) { result in
        asyncVideoCompositionRequest.finish
        (withComposedVideoFrame: destinationBuffer)
    }
}
```

This is an entry point to all the processing that is happening. Unlike MetalView, VideoCompositor wouldn't request a new frame for each screen update, so it has the disadvantage of a delay between the changing of the effect panel and a new rendering iteration.

Build and run your project. After these updates, all available effects should work fine, and edit the video frame. Figure 16-7 demonstrates the final output after processing a video frame with various effects applied.

Figure 16-7. *The final output of processed video frame with applied effects*

Conclusion

This chapter focused on how to process video frames with Metal. It covered converting YUV to RGB and applying real-time effects using a compute pipeline. The next chapter continues to explore video processing, and you learn how to overlay multiple videos, use them as layers, and combine them with image layers.

CHAPTER 17

Video Layers

The previous two chapters explored layer composition and customized video rendering by extending frame processing with Metal-driven filters and effects. Now, let's combine this knowledge to create a more complex layer rendering pipeline, enabling you to use videos as layers with various effects, blend modes, and transformations.

Understanding the Video Layers Rendering Pipeline

Rendering video layers involves similar stages to single video processing but with a different approach to achieve the same goals.

As mentioned in Chapter 16, the AVFoundation stage customizes the processing of each video frame. Unlike single video processing, layers are multiple, requiring a method to fetch the current video frame from each video layer asset in the pipeline. You'll solve this problem using AVComposition, which includes all layers stored in the composition by their track ID. By the end of this stage, all added video layers have an updated version of their video frame as a source texture.

In the Metal processing stage, layers with previously updated source textures are processed and rendered, similar to how image layers are handled in LayerRenderingTool. For more information on layer rendering, refer to Chapter 13.

© Bogdan Redkin and Victor Yaskevich 2024
B. Redkin and V. Yaskevich, *Master Photo and Video Editing with Metal*,
https://doi.org/10.1007/979-8-8688-0832-6_17

Setting up Video Layers

When a video asset is selected, the VideoContentLayerSurface is initialized to handle the video content as a layer. The VideoComposition actor stores each video layer as an instance of AVMutableCompositionTrack added to an instance of AVMutableComposition named composition.

Open the starter project and explore the steps in configuring the video layer. Let's begin by examining the addVideoLayer function in the VideoComposition actor.

```
func addVideoLayer(videoLayerSurface: VideoContentLayerSurface)
async throws {
    let tracks = try await videoLayerSurface.asset.loadTracks
    (withMediaType: .video)
    let trackId = CMPersistentTrackID(renderingTool.layers.
    count + 1)

    let scaleX = min(3.0, max(1.0 / (self.videoComposition.
    renderSize.width / videoLayerSurface.size.width), 0.0))
    let scaleY = min(3.0, max(1.0 / (self.videoComposition.
    renderSize.height / videoLayerSurface.size.height), 0.0))

    if let compositionTrack = composition.addMutableTrack
    (withMediaType: .video, preferredTrackID: trackId),
        let track = tracks.first {
        compositionTrack.preferredTransform = CGAffine
        Transform(scaleX: scaleX, y: scaleY)

        try compositionTrack.insertTimeRange(videoLayerSurface.
        timeRange, of: track, at: .zero)
        let layer = Layer(layer: videoLayerSurface)
```

```
    layer.transform = Transform(scale: .init(x:
    scaleX.float, y: scaleY.float))
    self.renderingTool.layers.append(layer)
  }
}
```

In this code snippet, a new instance of `VideoContentLayerSurface` calculates the scale relative to the current video composition render size. The track ID is generated based on the current count of layers. `trackId` adds a new instance of `AVMutableCompositionTrack` to the current composition. `compositionTrack` with `trackId` is connected to the index of the `videoContentLayerSurface` layer, allowing retrieval of the source frame by track ID.

After that, `videoLayerSurface` is added as a layer to `LayerRenderingTool`. This process is illustrated in Figure 17-1.

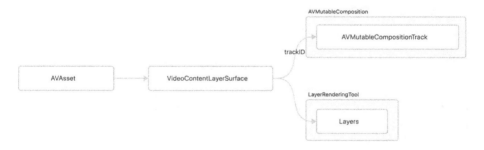

Figure 17-1. *Architecture of the video layers rendering pipeline*

Update the VideoCompositionInstruction Class

The `VideoCompositionInstruction` class is responsible for creating the list of required source track IDs. This list includes the track IDs of all the video content layers necessary for the composition.

To generate a list of required source track IDs, update the initialization method of VideoCompositionInstruction with the following code.

```
init(renderingTool: LayerRenderingTool, timeRange:
CMTimeRange) {
        self.timeRange = timeRange
        self.renderingTool = renderingTool
        self.requiredSourceTrackIDs = renderingTool.layers
            .enumerated()
            .filter({ $0.element.surface is VideoContent
              LayerSurface })
            .compactMap({ CMPersistentTrackID($0.offset + 1) })
            .filter({ $0 != kCMPersistentTrackID_Invalid })
            .compactMap({ $0 as NSValue })
    }
```

This code sets up the requiredSourceTrackIDs array by iterating through the renderingTool layers, filtering out those that are instances of VideoContentLayerSurface, and collecting their track IDs.

Update the Video Layers Source Texture to the Corresponding Video Frame

Storing a list of composition tracks with a track ID allows you to receive the video source frame for each added video layer.

Figure 17-2 illustrates this process.

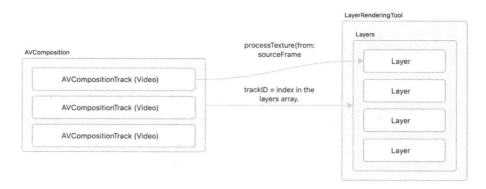

Figure 17-2. *The process of storing a list of composition tracks in layers*

Currently, the implementation of the startRequest function retrieves the source frame of the first track in compositionRequest, as shown in the following code snippet.

```
func startRequest(_ asyncVideoCompositionRequest:
AVAsynchronousVideoCompositionRequest) {
    guard
        let instruction = asyncVideoCompositionRequest.
        videoCompositionInstruction as?
        VideoCompositionInstruction,
        let commandBuffer = instruction.renderingTool.
        commandQueue.makeCommandBuffer(),
        let sourceFrame = asyncVideoCompositionRequest.
        sourceFrame(byTrackID: asyncVideoCompositionRequest.
        sourceTrackIDs[0].int32Value),
        //...
```

To iterate through the list of available source tracks and retrieve the source frame for each track, remove all usage of the old source frame, including locking and unlocking buffer address CVPixelBufferLockBaseAdd ress(sourceFrame, .readOnly) functions. Then, insert the following code.

```
asyncVideoCompositionRequest.sourceTrackIDs.forEach {
sourceTrackId in
    if let sourceFrame = asyncVideoCompositionRequest.
    sourceFrame(byTrackID: sourceTrackId.int32Value),
        let videoContentLayerSurface = instruction.
        renderingTool.layers[sourceTrackId.intValue - 1].surface
        as? VideoContentLayerSurface
    {
        CVPixelBufferLockBaseAddress(sourceFrame , .readOnly)
        videoContentLayerSurface.processTexture(from:
        sourceFrame, commandBuffer: commandBuffer)
        CVPixelBufferUnlockBaseAddress(sourceFrame, .readOnly)
    }
}
```

Build and run your project. You should be able to overlay multiple video layers in the same way as images. Figure 17-3 demonstrates the result of overlaying multiple video layers in the same way as image layers.

Figure 17-3. *Overlaying multiple video layers*

Conclusion

This chapter described integrating video layers into your rendering pipeline using Metal and AVFoundation. It covered setting up video layers, updating the `VideoCompositionInstruction` class, and handling multiple video frames.

APPENDIX

Common Metal Functions

Welcome to the appendix. Here, you will find descriptions and implementations of various Metal functions referenced throughout the book.

Creating a File with Shared Functions

Create a file named Color.h, which contains all the functions. Let's use the colors namespace for each item to keep the global namespace clean. Your file should look something like the following.

```
#ifndef Color_h
#define Color_h

#include <metal_stdlib>
using namespace metal;

namespace colors {
    // Here we will put all our shared items.
}

#endif
```

The upcoming sections explain the functions to add to this namespace.

© Bogdan Redkin and Victor Yaskevich 2024
B. Redkin and V. Yaskevich, *Master Photo and Video Editing with Metal*,
https://doi.org/10.1007/979-8-8688-0832-6

Using File with Shared Functions

To use the content of the shared file in your Metal shaders, you should import it as follows.

```
// NOTE: that path may be different in your project.
// You need to specify the path to the file you've created.
#include "../../Shaders/Colors.h"

void exampleFunction() {
    // Use `exampleSharedFunction` from our `colors` namespace.
    colors::exampleSharedFunction();
}
```

Shared Metal Functions

Convert Between RGB and HSL

The following functions perform a conversion between RGB and HSL. The specifics of the implementations are related to the definitions of HSL and RGB, which are beyond the scope of this book. Please note that all values in HSL are normalized to a [0; 1] range.

```
// Convert RGB color to HSL.
// All output values are in range [0; 1].
METAL_FUNC float3 rgbToHsl(float3 rgb) {
    float maxColor = max(max(rgb.r, rgb.g), rgb.b);
    float minColor = min(min(rgb.r, rgb.g), rgb.b);
    float delta = maxColor - minColor;

    float h = 0.0;
    float s = 0.0;
    float l = (maxColor + minColor) / 2.0;
```

```
    if (delta != 0) {
        s = (l < 0.5)
          ? (delta / (maxColor + minColor))
          : (delta / (2.0 - maxColor - minColor));

        if (rgb.r == maxColor) {
            h = (rgb.g - rgb.b) / delta
                + (rgb.g < rgb.b ? 6.0 : 0.0);
        } else if (rgb.g == maxColor) {
            h = (rgb.b - rgb.r) / delta + 2.0;
        } else {
            h = (rgb.r - rgb.g) / delta + 4.0;
        }

        h /= 6.0;
    }

    return float3(h, s, l);
}

// Convert HSL to linear RGB.
// Input HSL components must be in range [0; 1].
METAL_FUNC float3 hslToRgb(float3 hsl) {
    float h = hsl.x;
    float s = hsl.y;
    float l = hsl.z;

    float r, g, b;

    if (s == 0) {
        r = g = b = l; // achromatic
    } else {
        float q = l < 0.5 ? l * (1 + s) : l + s - l * s;
        float p = 2 * l - q;
```

```
        r = hueToRgb(p, q, h + 1.0/3.0);
        g = hueToRgb(p, q, h);
        b = hueToRgb(p, q, h - 1.0/3.0);
    }

    return float3(r, g, b);
}
```

Linear and Gamma sRGB Conversion

The following functions convert color from linear to gamma sRGB and vice versa.

```
// If x <= edge returns 1.0, otherwise 0.0 (component-wise).
METAL_FUNC float3 lessThan(float3 x, float3 edge) {
    return float3(x <= edge);
}

// Converts linear rgb to gamma rgb.
METAL_FUNC float3 linearToSRGB(float3 linear) {
    linear = clamp(linear, 0.0f, 1.0f);
    return mix(
        pow(linear * 1.055f, 1.0f / 2.4f) - 0.055f,
        linear * 12.92f,
        lessThan(linear, float3(0.0031308f))
    );
}
```

```
// Converts gamma rgb to linear rgb.
METAL_FUNC float3 SRGBToLinear(float3 rgb) {
    rgb = clamp(rgb, 0.f, 1.f);
    return mix(
        pow((rgb + 0.055f) / 1.055f, 2.4f),
        rgb / 12.92f,
        lessThan(rgb, 0.04045f)
    );
}
```

Index

A

Alpha blending, 220–222
Alpha compositing, 225–227
   opacity, 220
AngleFactor, 213
Apple's frameworks, 5
Application programming
   interface (API), 4
AVFoundation framework, 262
AVVideoComposition, 263–265

B

Bell-shaped function, 170
Blending, 227–229
Blend modes, 233
   hard light, 239–241
   Layer class, 231
   multiply, 233–236
   overlay, 238, 239
   screen, 236–238
Blur
   box, 168, 169
   convolution filter, 167
   convolution kernel, 167
   Gaussian function, 169–173
   GPU implementation, 173–175
   shader, 175–191

Box blur, 168, 169, 173
Buffers
   creation, 10
   MTL, 10

C

CATransform3D matrix, 82
Clip space coordinates, 49,
   57, 58, 66
   data type, 95
   4D homogeneous coordinate
     system, 95
   to NDC, 97, 101
   perspective division, 98
   structure, 96
   w dimension, 96–101
Color adjustments
   compute shaders, 139, 140
   image effect abstraction, 140
   image's contrast, brightness,
     and saturation
     shader, 140–151
   implementation, 147
Color burn, 243–245
Color coordinates calculation, 194
Compositing, 220, 221
Compute command encoders, 13

W, X

Y, Z

GPSR Compliance
The European Union's (EU) General Product Safety Regulation (GPSR) is a set
of rules that requires consumer products to be safe and our obligations to
ensure this.

If you have any concerns about our products, you can contact us on

ProductSafety@springernature.com

In case Publisher is established outside the EU, the EU authorized
representative is:

Springer Nature Customer Service Center GmbH
Europaplatz 3
69115 Heidelberg, Germany